The Day
After
He Left
for Iraq

The Day After He Left for Iraq

A STORY OF LOVE, FAMILY & REUNION

Melissa Seligman

Skyhorse Publishing

Skyhorse Publishing books may be purchased in bulk at special discounts for sales promotion, corporate gifts, fund raising, or educational purposes. Special editions can also be created to specifications. For details, contact the Special Sales Department, Skyhorse Publishing, 555 Eighth Avenue, Suite 903, New York, NY 10018 or info@skyhorsepublishing.com.

www.skyhorsepublishing.com

10 9 8 7 6 5 4 3 2 1

Library of Congress Cataloging-in-Publication Data

Seligman, Melissa.
    The day after he left for Iraq : a story of love, family & reunion / Melissa Seligman.
        p. cm.
    ISBN 978-1-60239-294-6
    1. Iraq War, 2003- 2. Seligman, Melissa. 3. Military spouses--United States--Biography. 4. Military spouses--United States--Conduct of life. I. Title.
    DS79.76.S4516 2008
    956.7044'31--dc22
    [B]
                                        2008025981

Interior design by LeAnna Weller Smith
Printed in the United States of America

This book is dedicated to

Amelia and Elijah
for always holding my hand

And David
for always holding my heart

Contents

Death

"Maybe I'll even confess the truth."

—Barbara Kingsolver, *The Poisonwood Bible*

A Painful Goodbye

3:25 a.m. November 5, 2005.

When the first bomb explodes, it takes nearly three seconds for the thundering sound to reach my ears. Fire tears through the streets of Baghdad while men and women run, screaming. The sky is clouded with purple haze as the smoke begins to snake its way through the cold night air. The smell of burnt flesh fills my nose, and I search the street for some sign of my husband. Soldiers rush past me, their brown desert boots pounding the pavement. "Run! Take cover!" they shout as they push stunned people to the ground and make their way through the parked cars, all the while scanning the streets and rooftops with their guns. I try to run with them, but my bare feet are buried in the crumbled pavement.

Bullets rip through the air, tearing and piercing bodies as white fills the sky, followed by red flames in the distance. Still no sign of his face, but his mumbled voice echoes in the distance. Over and over again, he calls my name. Cold hands wrap around my pajama-clad body, and a violent scream finally pushes its way through my lips and into the smoke-filled haze of war.

"Are you okay? Hey! Wake up!"

I snap awake to find his knowing eyes staring into my own. Tears slide down my cheeks and disappear into my wet pillow. His hands hold my face while my racing mind tries to relax and listen to his soothing words. "Calm down. It was just a dream," he says. When my breathing finally slows, he pulls my face to his and kisses my damp forehead. He doesn't ask what the dream was about. He doesn't have to.

6:25: My husband is leaving for Iraq today.

How can I say goodbye to him? Is there a way? I try to say goodbye quietly, loudly, nonchalantly, and angrily. Nothing seems to feel like goodbye. Everything seems to feel like goodbye.

We have been preparing for this for nine months. I found out I was pregnant just before he received his orders to leave us. Again. He is only doing a soldier's job, and his job involves war. Still, how many times can he leave us? How many goodbyes are in us? No amount of preparation for goodbye can ever lessen the blow of him leaving. There is no way to prepare for him to never come home from war. And with a raw, protruding, unprepared heart, I search for a way to force myself to stay behind as he turns to walk away. My mind plays constant images of our impending separation in hopes of lessening the pain of goodbye. Or forcing the breaking day back into the darkness of night. All in vain.

When the sun comes into our window, it feels cold and lonely. Our eight-week-old cries out. How do you tell a baby goodbye?

My husband is quiet next to me as he cuddles our son in the curve of his body and whispers in his ear. The newborn cries soften, and turn to cooing. My husband begins humming softly, and the mattress moves with his swaying body. Blankly, I stare at the wall and beg my stomach to calm.

Our twenty-two-month-old daughter is waking. She calls from her room, "Daddy! Daddy! I get up now." I pull the covers over my head and bury my face in the pillow. My chest is tight. With no way

4

to contain them, a few tears leave my eyes. When she calls for him tomorrow, he will be gone.

I roll over and meet his eyes. "Do you want me to go get her?" I ask. He doesn't. He is only waiting to hear her say "Daddy" again. When she calls for him again, he hands me the baby, gets up slowly, and walks into her room. Our son snuggles against my chest as my husband forces himself to fake happiness in her room. She doesn't seem to notice his façade.

6:30: I cry.

6:35: I am angry.

6:40: I hold him.

6:45: I nurse his son.

6:50: I play with his daughter.

6:55: I cry.

7:00: I smile. I have to send him off with a smile. I hide in the bathroom and cry. I hide in the laundry room and cry. The sound of the clothes moving through the dryer muffles my sobs.

8:00: In the living room, my mother is already awake. She has been here for weeks helping with the baby and offering unending support. Her eyes are wet and swollen. She has been crying, but she quickly wipes the evidence from her face. My eyes meet hers for only a moment before I look away. I can't break. No words pass between us. The usual morning greetings seem useless.

9:00: I fix his favorite breakfast. We all gather around the table for his last meal, and I wonder how he feels. Can he taste it? Is he able to swallow past the lump in his throat? The food on my plate looks repulsive, but I force myself to eat. If I give in to this hovering depression, he will feel guilty for leaving. He has to know I am strong. He needs to see it. His strength shines as he plays with Amelia while she eats. Amelia laughs as he pretends to fall from his chair. "Again," she says. He obliges. My mother and I attempt to join in the fun. We fall short. Elijah is sleeping again.

10:30: My husband checks and rechecks his bags. He is nervous, scared, anxious, hesitant. I want to calm him. I want to help him. I want nothing to do with him.

12:30: My husband puts Amelia down for a nap. His voice flows through the monitor and into the living room. "I have to go to work, baby. I won't be back for a while." He stops short. His voice is breaking. "You have to be a good girl for Mommy, okay? Can you do that for me? Can you be a good girl for me and help her with your brother?"

"Daddy go to work?" she asks. Quietly he answers, "Yeah. I'm just going to work. I will miss you and think of you every second." He moans softly, and I know he is holding her and crying. He is trying to convince himself that he is a good father and that leaving doesn't make him a bad father. He is trying.

She doesn't understand. How could a toddler possibly understand? She tells him, "Bye," and asks him for her dolls.

12:45: I go into the garage to cry.

12:46: I hold my husband in the garage while he sobs. "She won't forget you. And he will always know you. No matter what happens," I whisper in his ear. He says nothing. "I am so proud of you." He pulls away and looks into my eyes. He nods. "I love you so much," I tell him as my hands move over his face, his hair, his arms, his hands. "I love you, too."

I love him. Somehow those words cannot capture it. I am inside of him.

1:00: My mother and I sit in silence on the couch while he runs one last errand. I want to talk to her. My mind clings to some hope that she can explain this to me, take it from me, or help me in some way. But there is no help. No amount of words could take this away.

Cold November rain pounds on the living room windows as she puts her delicate hand over mine. "I don't know how you did this last time by yourself. Waiting around all day to say goodbye. This feels like going to a funeral," she says quietly. I force myself to look at her. My tears finally fall.

"Thank you for being here, Momma." I stop myself. I can't tell her I am terrified he is going to die or that I refuse to tell him goodbye. My heart feels heavy and dead. She knows. She squeezes my hand and wipes away my tears. We sit in silence, lost in our thoughts.

2:00: One hour until he leaves. I run frantically through the house searching for something of mine, some part of me, to give him. Something personal. Something delicate. I am angry with myself. I should have planned and prepared to send him off with the perfect gift.

I claw through my dresser, searching for a perfect something. There is nothing. Only comfortable and maternal underwear. My hand stumbles across a yellow handkerchief. David loves hand-kerchiefs. He considers them timeless and romantic. This one was given to me when I was a bridesmaid at a friend's wedding. My name is sewn in green with curly, graceful letters. My hands move over the lace edges, and I hold the soft material to my face. I spray my favorite perfume onto the fabric, walk to the bed, and place it inside one of the many pockets of his uniform.

3:00: My husband packs our truck with his gear. He has packed it numerous times now. He was originally supposed to leave seven weeks ago. But his goodbye got pushed back, day by day, and then week by week. Each week brought fresh joy as we realized he would

7

have more time with us, but also pain that our goodbyes would continue without end or certainty. But this goodbye feels solid. With the plane fueled and ready, we know he is finally leaving. While Amelia naps under Granna's watch, Elijah and I take my husband to a building, some building. It is some building that I should know. I am not a good Army wife, not by my neighbors' standards and not by his commander's standards. At some point, Army and wife became incongruent. I am now sharing my husband with an unspeakable and unidentified presence. It engulfs us. Its seduction is demonic. It threatens to sleep with my husband and to carry his soul away from us. Now there is only the sound of pounding rain and straining blades pushing across the windshield. His hand rests on my knee.

3:25: I sob quietly and violently as he pulls Elijah out of the truck to hold him one last time. I wrap my arms around my chest to calm my pounding heart, while he smells Elijah and softly strokes his face. He pulls him close and again whispers in his ear.

"His skin is so soft. He has no idea what is happening," he says through clenched teeth. "Kiss him for me. Will you do that?" he asks quietly. I nod.

3:30: He puts on his gear. It is gear I do not understand. He wants to tell me what it is for. I try not to imagine what it is for. I can't hug him enough. I can't kiss him enough. What if this is the last kiss? How should the last kiss feel? How should a last hug sound? There are no words. I can only stare into his eyes, push myself to allow him to leave, and plead silently. Please, my sweet, sweet husband, come home to me.

3:35: I stand in the rain in the middle of the parking lot of some building. I am not a good Army wife. He walks toward the bus and falls in with the other waiting soldiers. I lose him in the sea of desert brown. They all look the same. They all seem excited and scared and worried and sad. I taste rain and tears.

Dying

The bus pulls away, and I search for his face through the blurry windows. Steamy hands press against the windows, and I wave, hoping that one of those hands is his. Standing in the parking lot with wet hair, wet cheeks, and a memory of his arms around my waist, I am numb. I try to remember our last words.

"Promise me that you will take care of yourself," I begged him. "You aren't going to Afghanistan this time. Don't lie to me and tell me that this security job you are working isn't dangerous." He shuffles from foot to foot and avoids my probing eyes. "The new equipment you got for this job, will it protect you?" I ask, trying to persuade my brain that his gear is magical, and he will be left untouched.

"This is the best. Don't worry. I'm too stubborn for anything to happen," he says. "I love you. I love you more every day. Always remember that," he demands. He pulls me close to him. My arms can hardly reach around his bulletproof vest. The smell of oil and metal fills my nose.

"I have to go. I won't look back. I can't," he says as he holds my wet face in his rough gloves. "Give me a smile," he says. I force my lips apart and attempt a smile. He returns the favor. He kisses my lips softly, and turns to walk away. I want him to look back. Just to see his face one last time. Instead, I cherish the taste of his lips on mine.

I replay his words to me over and over again. I need to remember his voice, his hands on my face as he begs one last smile from me. I hate myself for letting him go. I should have held him longer. Maybe if I had, my arms wouldn't feel so empty now.

I turn and walk back to our truck. My truck now. Elijah is secured in his car seat. He is the only witness to my sadness. He listens to me beg God to keep David safe, to bring him home to me, to keep him strong, and to keep me strong. He coos quietly while I convulse with tears. The ache in my chest is painful. It is sharp and relentless. The goodbyes never get easier. The pain never dulls. It will never matter how many times he has left before; the weight of goodbye still collapses my chest.

There has to be a way to push the pain aside, to make it run in fear, to be a fortress. Otherwise I risk falling into a terrifying canyon filled with glimpses of his destruction or images of him in a coffin. I need to cut my heart from my chest to ensure that I never fully feel the pain of telling him goodbye again. Maybe for the last time.

I want to be made of steel. To be constructed of hinges and metal scraps and incapable of identifying the anguish in my daughter's eyes when she realizes her father has left again. My chest tightens and my heart pounds as I imagine her screaming his name. Thoughts of Elijah pushing David away when he returns because he does not know his father bring stinging, fresh tears to my eyes. I have to find a way to shield my babies from all this intensity and sadness.

I try to bring myself back to the present and avoid my certain future. To listen to my son laughing. He is content and oblivious, and I am thankful he is at peace in his car seat rather than in my unsteady, shaking arms. My entire body trembles.

I try to shove the fact that he is gone into the corners of my mind. I am alone. I am alone. I am alone. I need to find a way to believe it. I can't think of his lingering kiss on my lips. I don't want to smell him in the seat next to me. I try not to see him in the rear-view mirror. He isn't there anymore.

My trembling hands move the gearshift through the gears as I push myself to drive away from the cold, wet parking lot. Tears cloud my eyes, and I force myself to hold them at bay, just until I find our driveway again. Everything feels mechanical, and I pull onto our street without fully realizing just how I got there. When the sound of the engine dies, and we are safely home, I drop my head onto the steering wheel and release every tear I have been holding back.

I search the truck for David's cell phone, my phone now. My closest friend answers my call, and I fall into heaving sobs when her familiar voice fills my ears. She has been expecting me, and she doesn't ask how I am doing. She doesn't ask anything. She only listens to my staccato breathing until I manage to regain control. "I can't do this. I'm not strong enough for this. I can't bear the thought of my life without him," I cry into the phone. She says nothing.

I cry for what feels like hours. Only minutes have passed. Time seems to have stalled on this moment. My breathing begins to return to normal, and my tears begin to slow. "I need to go in. I'm sure Amelia is up by now, and I need to pull myself together. Thanks," I say as she quietly tells me she loves me and ends the call.

I force my feet to the ground, and I open Elijah's door to find his tiny hands poking out from the car seat cover. His blue hat has fallen over his eyes, and when I pull it away, he looks at me with such love and innocence. His eyes steady me for the moment, and my hands stop shaking as I bend into the truck to greet him. "Hey, little man. Ready to go in?" I ask. His toothless grin draws a smile from me as I pull the release to free his car seat and situate the awkward load against my hip.

My mother greets us when we come through the door. Her eyes are swollen from crying. She doesn't say anything. She continues to show the grace and compassion she has freely given for weeks. She has been strong, comforting, empathetic, and heartbroken. She has been a mother. She wants to hold me. I don't let her.

Amelia runs to me. "Mommy, you home! I good sleeper for Granna. Where's Daddy?" she asks. My eyes search the room for an answer. They beg the walls for some sense of commanding direction. My mother sits quietly on the couch. Her eyes are full of sympathy and concern. And she refuses to allow one tear to spill onto her cheek. She holds my stare and says nothing.

"Daddy is at work. He made you something special, though. Want to see it?" I ask. "Yeah!" she screams. I walk to the television and search for the tape David made for the kids. My hands shake as I pull it from the casing, and I close my eyes, remembering when he first decided to make it. His voice echoes in my head.

"I want them to remember me as their daddy, not a soldier in a stiff uniform," he said. "She always thinks it's funny when I fall. Do you think I should film myself falling?" He never listened for my answer. His mind was too busy constructing a video full of happy images for his children. "I just want to make sure that they are smiling when they watch it."

I filmed him playing with the soccer ball and zoomed in on his feet as he gave specific directions about how to correctly dribble the ball. "Don't ask Mommy for help with the soccer ball, babies. She doesn't understand how to make the ball part of your feet." On camera, I pretended to be insulted as I held back tears.

We sat in the living room as he sang songs about clapping hands and stomping feet. He read aloud from colorful books about puppies, caterpillars, and beautiful butterflies. He played hide-and-seek with the camera as he called their names throughout the house. I managed to keep the camera steady while he laughed, fell, played, and read for his babies. The video is a solid hour—enough to keep them entertained in short bursts for months.

His beautiful voice fills the room now, as I hit play. Amelia watches her father pretend to fall. She laughs. She watches him kick a soccer ball. She admires. She watches and listens as he reads her favorite book. His tone is expressive and tender. He reads the worn book to her as if it is the first time. She follows. He talks sweetly and happily into the camera. She meets his stare with complete adoration. Next to her, Elijah turns his head toward his daddy's voice. I smile and think of the countless hours David spent talking softly into his ear. "I'm scared he won't recognize my voice when I call home," he'd said.

"That will never happen," I promised him.

Every nerve inside me claws its way to the surface. My mind tells me to stand strong and to stay in this moment with my babies. Amelia's laughter should be enough to get me through the heartache of hearing his voice. But it isn't. I go to the bathroom and try to hold myself in. I wrap my arms around my chest and beg my stomach to stop churning and lurching. It revolts into the toilet. I look at what will be my final act of weakness, and flush.

In the mirror my eyes are vacant and lifeless. It feels as though I am no longer here. I am somewhere on a crowded plane, holding David's hand and looking to Baghdad. Here feels cold and empty without him. Here feels void of life. But here is my reality.

I take inventory. I spend nearly the full hour, as his voice entertains our children, persuading myself to be who I need to be. Mother. Father. Nurse. Counselor. Clown. Confidant.

I create my armor out of hate, out of love, out of fear, out of self-loathing, and out of respect. It is the only way I will survive. Until he calls, e-mails, or sends letters, my husband, my children's father, my best friend, does not exist.

The Empty Seat

The first night without him is unbearable. Dreams of repeated goodbyes and an uncertain future plague me. We are back there, in that same parking lot with the rain and the tears. He walks away from me again and again. He turns, only for a moment, but he has no face. Nothing fills his helmet. The same dream haunts me throughout the night.

I wake from a fitful sleep. Elijah sleeps soundly next to me, and I feel his radiating warmth. Today is his eight-week baby appointment. Amelia will be waking soon. My chest aches to think of explaining his absence to her.

My bare feet sting from the freezing floor, and I tiptoe across the room to find my clothes for the day. The sun is shining, but our house is cold. Another upstate New York winter is hovering on the horizon. I dread the frigid days and nights to come.

"Daddy!" Amelia calls. She asks for him every morning. He is the center of her world. Everyone else is scenery. Even when he has been gone for months of training, she still asks for him. She never

gives up hope that he will be the one to walk into the room, smiling
and lifting her from her crib.

I open the door and walk across her colorful shag rug, and I
instantly think of David, carrying it over his shoulder the day we
bought it. He unrolled it on the hard, bare floor of the room that was
to become her nursery. I can still feel his hands rubbing my enormous belly. "Do you think he or she will like it?" he'd asked. "What's
not to like? It's colorful and soft. It will be a perfect place to crawl,"
I'd said. We had no way of knowing that she would sit, roll, crawl,
and run everywhere but on that rug.

Now, she stands and bounces in her white crib that David and
I spent hours painting. The little stenciled green frogs and purple turtles stare at me from every angle. Everything in this room
reminds me of life with him. The pictures on the wall, the dresser
he painted, the shelf he hung above her crib, and the changing table
he so painstakingly put together. All representing the family we
started together.

She stops bouncing for the moment and looks to me for an
explanation as to why I have entered her room this morning instead
of David. "Good morning, sweet pea!" I say with a fake smile. She is
disappointed. "Want Daddy," she says. I explain, "Daddy isn't here
right now, baby. Daddy had to go to work." It is all I know to tell her.
She seems satisfied and reaches for me instead.

My eyes burn. My chest tightens. I try not to cry. Tears roll down
my cheeks, fall onto her rug, and I berate my body for betraying me.
She wraps her arms around my neck, and I hold her as long as she
will allow, then put her down. She runs from her room in search of
her toys and her chocolate milk. My mother cheerfully talks to her in
the living room; she has found enough to satisfy her for now.

Elijah cries his tiny newborn squeal. I go to him, lift him from
the bed, and smell his pink, soft skin. I cannot help but think of
the numerous times I watched David cuddle his newborn son. He
pushed his fingers into the soles of Elijah's feet just to watch his
little toes curl around them.

I pull Elijah close and uncover his delicate feet. Images of David
fill me. I see David kissing Elijah's new, pink feet. I see him in the

hospital, just after Elijah was born. I am in the bed, exhausted and thrilled, and David sits in the chair, kissing each of Elijah's toes. Elijah's booties are on the floor as David bathes him. He lingers on his tiny feet, tickles them and then delicately rinses the soap from them. "I just love his little toes. His feet are like little monkey feet," he says somewhere in the back of my mind. I swallow the lump in my throat and beg my shell to harden.

Elijah cries and nudges me, hungry. We cuddle on the bed and I will my convulsing breathing to slow, to relax enough for my milk to drop. I close my eyes and concentrate on the tiny fingers that curl around mine. I listen to his cry and think of the satisfaction that only I can give. The milk begins to flow, and he is content.

When he is finished eating, I walk into the living room to find Amelia on my mother's lap. I greet her warmly and begin making breakfast. At least, warming something up. I have little desire to cook a large breakfast with no David here to applaud my efforts. I still have to bundle Elijah, get him to the doctor, and attempt to make it home before the need to nurse sets in yet again.

With a waffle in Amelia's hand, and my mother happily munching on toast, I leave them to their world of puzzles, books, and toys. I zip Elijah under his car seat cover and situate his carrier on my hip. When I open the door, frigid air immediately chaps my cheeks and brings stinging tears to my eyes.

Elijah coos and giggles in the back of the truck as I drive the familiar roads to the clinic. David and I have driven this route so many times, and I ache for him to be here with me yet again. He loves to mark the babies' growth and enjoys each checkup he is able to make. Because he is forced to leave us, he always pushes himself to show up every time he can. So far, he has only missed two regular baby appointments, and I hate knowing he will miss more. His involvement in our lives is so intricate; the empty seat beside me solidifies the burning realization that he is gone.

When we reach the clinic, I step back out into the cold, pull Elijah's carrier from the backseat, and walk into the hallways full of Army men and women and wives. In the waiting areas, women stare into space, all with the same look of emptiness. They are surrounded by their children, and they are continuing to live, to breathe, but their hearts are somewhere else. You can see it in their eyes. And you can see the happiness to be home in the eyes of the soldiers seated next to their wives. The unbridled emotions of this war all swarm the air, mingle, and disperse tension throughout the halls. I feel overwhelmed.

When we finally reach the doctor, I am ready to explode. The doctor and I talk about Elijah's growing belly, his nursing habits, his dirty diapers, his healing belly button, and I begin to overflow with thoughts about David. "My husband is going to be so upset that he wasn't here for this. He always loves these visits." My comments catch her off guard. She stares at me for a moment before she recognizes the look on my face. "He hates it when he is gone. He is just such a good daddy. Always so involved. So caring. Just the kind of daddy you want for your kids, you know?" She nods her head in agreement and moves her stool closer to me.

Her knowing hand covers mine. It is warm, and the gentle squeeze she gives me urges more from my mouth. "He just loves newborn babies. The way they smell." The words tumble out of my mouth, and I have little control over my wandering mind. I desperately search for some shred of a normal conversation, but nothing about this pain feels normal. She pulls her hand from mine and moves it to my shoulder. Her quiet understanding and patience invite more from me, and my flooded mind breaks the dam I have attempted to create. "He likes to put them in those front carriers and vacuum. Isn't that silly?" I spill. Tears flow from my eyes, and she says nothing. Images of him laughing with the kids and carrying them in a sling while we shop attack my mind and leave me reeling. "Oh God," I breathe, "I just hope they know how much he loves them."

Her arm tightens around my shoulder as I begin to realize I have lost control. My mind travels back to the stark white office as David walks away, back into my memories. Her eyes are filled with concern, and I attempt some shred of composure. "I'm sorry. I'm so sorry. I didn't mean to turn this into a crying session about my husband. He just left for Iraq, so I'm a basketcase." I wipe the tears from my eyes and avoid her imploring stare. Embarrassed and ready to leave, I fumble with Elijah's clothes and begin putting him back into his carrier. "So, everything seems fine with Elijah?" I ask in some attempt to change the subject. She nods, hands me his new statistics, and holds the door for me as I mumble an apology. She says nothing as I walk into the hallway and back into the waiting room.

As I leave the clinic, I walk past men in uniform waiting with their children, waiting to get medicine, or wearing stethoscopes as they pop their heads out to call their next patient. David is in all of them. His boots. His uniform. His beret. I see him everywhere, and I wonder if there will ever be a way for him to know how much I miss him.

In Memory Of

Before we reach the truck, Elijah is already squealing. We were in the clinic too long. He is hungry, and my body won't wait until we get home. My shirt is already wet, and my milk is flowing freely. I start the truck, let it warm, and pull him from his car seat to nurse him. As he eats greedily, I look into his tiny, newborn face, and I see Amelia just after David left us nearly two years ago. I was in this exact same situation after her eight-week-old appointment.

That deployment, David walked out our kitchen door into the freezing February snow at one o'clock in the morning, leaving me and our six-week-old infant for close to three months. We had just moved to Fort Drum, and we knew he would be joining his unit to finish their already lengthy deployment. I should have been thankful that he only had to go for a short time.

It was only nine months after our wedding when I found out I was pregnant, and David had just left us for nearly seven months of training. He returned as a specialist in the Army. He missed nearly my entire pregnancy, and we tried to make the best of it. I should have appreciated that he was granted permission to stay behind from his deployment long enough for the birth of our new baby. But, having just been reunited, it was hard to tell him goodbye again. Unlike many soldiers, he did see her birth, and he helped me move to New York, but I could not reconcile watching him leave us. Not when we had just become a family. That was too much to ask.

That horrible night, he held his new daughter, cried for what he would miss with us, and turned to leave. I fell onto the floor and dry-heaved. I felt all of my security being purged out of me. I had no concept of what to expect while he was in Afghanistan. No idea exactly what war meant. And no idea what a new baby required. I had no clue how to be a mother when I had only just learned to be a wife. Much less an Army wife.

He reluctantly left me in a new home with a new baby, who seemed to scream all the time. She was full of piercing, deafening screams. I didn't know what to do with her or how to calm her.

In the truck, nursing our second newborn, alone and without him again, I feel all the same pain. Instantly I am there again, on the floor, waiting for him to come home and terrified that may never happen. I was alone, cold, and miserable as I listened to my new baby scream for comfort. I couldn't understand what more I could give her. Now, looking again at Elijah, it won't happen again. Amelia taught me well.

Weeks became months of Amelia being colicky. We couldn't get outside because the snow fell relentlessly. I was alone with a crying baby. He called every day. Sometimes twice a day. He wanted desperately to be part of us, but I had nothing to say. I didn't know how to tell him that I didn't think I liked her. I hated motherhood and I wanted to go back to just the two of us. I didn't know how to tell him anything, so I told him nothing. Instead, we talked about the physical changes in our new baby, I listened to his stories of missions, he listened to my ramblings about snow and nursing, and I pushed the depression and loneliness deep inside me.

After two months of cold darkness I stepped out into the light. No one came out to greet me. I introduced myself to this new way of life and desolate area: I am alone. I am scared. I am Melissa. No one answered. I stepped back inside to what had become my reality. Amelia and I were alone. We simply functioned. Nothing more.

At last Amelia melted me. She finally gave in to a routine with a rhythm full of melodic caresses and kiss-filled cuddle sessions. Her smiles found the cracks in my façade. Her small fingers curled around mine with a distinct delicacy. She wanted me to touch her. She wanted me to hold her. She laughed when I smiled at her. We began to groove to our own music and learned our own dance. It was one built out of mutual respect and necessity. She became my friend and confidant. She was no longer just a screaming baby to me. We were stuck in it together, and together we faced the bitter cold that finally gave way to budding trees and flowering lawns.

Spring brought David's return. He had a gun when Amelia and I went to get him. He picked up my daughter, my friend, while holding this gun. No one seemed to notice or care that a child was in one arm and a machine gun was in another. Worry clouded my mind to see the two together, but I said nothing. I assumed it was just my frayed nerves. He held her awkwardly. He was more comfortable holding his gun.

He was different; distant, cold. I was different, too; overly sensitive, bitter, tired. I was a mother. I had to learn how to be a wife again. My house was suddenly our house again. He was holding Amelia the wrong way and I reprimanded him. It was all wrong. Nothing about him felt right.

Yet she loved him. She fell naturally into his arms. Seeing her cuddle with him on the couch while my arms felt empty and cold made me crazy with jealousy. I had to work tirelessly for that affection. He didn't earn it. He didn't fight for it. He didn't calm her endless nights by singing, praying, and kissing. He didn't do anything but leave us. A stranger held my baby, my friend.

I didn't want to share anything with him. Only I had earned the right to call her mine. Everything in that house belonged to me. My baby. My house. My struggle. My marriage. My anger. He held my anger so tightly. In my opinion, he deserved no say in anything. How could he? His partnership had become null and void in my world.

Days turned to weeks. We were settled. He began to remember how to belong to our family. I began to forget why I married him. He fell in next to me. But I didn't need him anymore. I tried not to leave him. I tried to remember that he was my husband and Amelia's father and that he was the same person I fell in love with years ago. He had the same hands, the same heart, and the same smile. I'd pushed it all out of my heart in order to exist in his absence. The anger kept me alone in my world where I felt safe with Amelia.

I packed my things and Amelia's things. We would leave. He took himself from us. He left us. He left me. I wanted him to feel the pain of watching me walk away from him, and I needed him to hurt the same way I had hurt. Revenge propelled me, but the look on his face as I tried to drive away with my baby stopped me. In the rearview mirror, standing in the driveway, was my broken, sweet husband, and I realized that I had a choice he didn't have. I could stay and make this family work. I chose to turn around. Finally, I exhaled a long awaited, bated breath and gave in.

I still feel the pain of that deployment, the sense of abandonment and loss. And now, here we are, a year and a half later, once again in the same situation; the same lonely, horrifying, emotionally draining situation. Of course, now there are three of us left behind.

Elijah finishes nursing and falls into a deep sleep. My breath pulls in as I begin once again to stand on my own. I look forward to exhaling again. To letting go again. To choosing this family again.

Denial

"Her former and present lives
were so different that she couldn't
even hold one in her mind
as she lived the other."

—Barbara Kingsolver, *Prodigal Summer*

Rearview Mirrors

David left two days ago, and it is time to take my mother home. The kids and I are going, too, for the holidays. I don't want to watch the kids open gifts without David. But I am worried if we stay in New York, I will cheat my children of happiness that they deserve. If we stay in New York, I will refuse to celebrate. So we take off for Kentucky.

Even though I know my family offers comfort, I don't want to leave the house that has become my home. I can still smell David here. He still feels close to me here. He feels vibrant here. I feel surrounded by him in our empty bed. The dent from his body is still there.

My mother and I load my truck full of baby clothes, baby beds, food, diapers, and Pull-Ups. We spend hours packing, and when the sun sets, we decide to leave in hopes of Amelia sleeping through the drive. We have hours ahead of us.

We drive for sixteen hours, stopping only for me to nurse Elijah. He is content to sleep away the night. But Amelia refuses to sleep.

She sits in her seat chattering like we are on a grand adventure. She only sleeps for thirty minutes of the trip. She can feel a change in the air.

I pass the driving time by singing about squishing bumble bees and bus horns beep, beep, beeping and by babbling to my mother. "You know, by the time we go back to New York, we will only have about eight months left. That really isn't that bad," I talk at her. "We will just have to keep busy doing fun things." My mother says nothing, only nods. She can hear the desperation in my voice. "I just have to bury myself in the kids. Just totally forget this is happening and keep my focus on them." I stare at the lines on the road and push myself to believe it. I am fooling no one. My mother shakes her head at me and smiles.

We arrive at my childhood home at eleven in the morning. We are completely exhausted. My body aches, and my mother can hardly keep her eyes open. We are both cranky and desperate to escape the confines of my truck. Amelia is the only one chipper and excited. We pull into the driveway, and Amelia screams with delight. "Papa! I here Papa!" she yells through the truck window.

My older brother has come over during his lunch hour to see us, and he and my father greet us with strong hugs. My dad asks about the drive and tells us that he hardly slept because he was so worried. "Well, nobody slept in this truck except Elijah," I say, half laughing. No one mentions David. No one discusses what could become of him. No one wants to admit what is happening.

My father reaches for Elijah and cups him in his strong arms. This is their first meeting. He'd come to witness the birth, but had to leave to return to work when Elijah refused to come out. My father holds him with pride and talks about how long he has waited to meet Elijah. My brother picks up Amelia and swings her high in the air. She giggles with pleasure and he pulls her to his chest in a gentle bear hug. While my brother's strong arms hold her, I think of David's arms swinging her through the air while she screams, "More, Daddy!" He always gave more when she asked. I try to focus on the men who have my babies now, and not the one who can't hold them.

Melissa Seligman

I begin to unload the truck to still my wandering mind. The house smells familiar. It smells quaint. It is calm and quiet. But it doesn't smell like home. I can't smell him here. I can't see his last shower. I can't hear his laughter. I know that I am safe here. I can cry if I need to. I can laugh if I want to. I can scream if anyone would care to listen.

They do care. They care deeply. They miss him, too. I can tell by what they don't say that my mother and my father are concerned about me and him. They don't know what to say. This is the first time my family has been around me when David is deployed. When he left for Afghanistan, they only talked to me on the phone. They are in new territory having me in front of them. They can see my fragile state. They can feel my tense demeanor. I'm on the edge and I'm thankful they can see the dynamite around me.

I don't speak his name. I can't. I am afraid. I am terrified to break my fragile bubble and unleash my insanity. Instead I say nothing of my heartache and nothing of the fissure in my chest.

He is somewhere in the air right now. He is somewhere traveling in this world, and I feel so distant from everything that feels like him. In my parents' house, I don't see his uniforms in the closet. I can't smell his boot polish. Here, he has no shampoo, and he has no razors.

Tears will only be met with pity here. Hugs will only bring pain. In New York, I can suffer in silence. In New York, few people know my name. I can screen calls there. I can sink into a world where love, pain, agony, war, and marriage no longer exist. In New York, other wives suffer and yearn next to me in silence and complete understanding. Here, I will be greeted with love and open discussions about my pain. Here, people will want to help me. And I can't allow that. Not yet. Accepting help means admitting he is gone. And I just can't do that.

Instead I choose to accept the hugs that are offered and thank my family for having me. I don't tell them I am destroyed. I only smile and talk about the weeks to come. Perhaps thinking ahead will keep me from looking behind to everything I have walked away from. If I try to look in front of me, maybe I won't see him standing behind me, waiting for me to come home.

Thanks Given

The month of November continues to drag. I fill each day with endless activities and attempt to avoid his absence. Little is said about the deployment, and I try to find joy and happiness in my friends and family. But each moment spent with them causes my mind to reel and concoct images of times past. Of laughing moments. Of cold morning snuggle sessions and freezing feet on David's back. Everywhere I look, there is an imprint of him. So I try to look nowhere.

But today, I have to look toward his parents' house. It is Thanksgiving, and I want the kids to have dinner with David's family. But I dread seeing them. They all look like him. They all sound like him. They remind me of everything him, but I know he would want me there.

All morning is spent packing myself and the kids for the drive to Louisville. I have everything I could possibly need. Diapers. Bibs. Pull-Ups. Extra clothes. Toys. Drinks. Sippy cups. Hopefully my first trip alone with my children will be uneventful and smooth. I am scared to drive alone with them. What if Elijah starts crying? What if I need to nurse him before I get to Louisville? What if the truck breaks down? My mind spins as I think about all that could go wrong. I know that I am not the first parent to drive nearly three hours alone, so I leave my parents' house in Corbin with a smile and tuck my fears into the corners of my mind.

The first few minutes of the trip are fabulous. Amelia is humming along to music, and Elijah is already giving in to the lulling movement of the truck. We merge onto the interstate, and I breathe a sigh of relief. Few people are on the road today. They are somewhere basting turkeys and smelling thick familial smells. It is a beautiful sunny day, and I feel a grin on my face as I realize my worries were unfounded.

"Mommy!" Amelia screams from the backseat. I look into the rearview mirror and see her furrowed brow. "What, baby? What do you need?" I ask. She doesn't respond. She says nothing, but she begins to whine. When she first starts, it is tolerable. But then, her voice begins to change tones, and her whines turn from a low moan to high-pitched screeching sounds.

"Amelia! Stop! Why are you screaming?" I ask her over my shoulder. "Mommy!" she screams. "You have to calm down, baby," I say. I try to concentrate on the road in front of me, but her cries cause the hairs on my neck to stand, and an instant pain begins to shoot across my forehead and into my temples. Elijah is crying. I feel like crying.

"Mommy!" she wails one last time before her mouth opens and she begins to gag. Her eyes roll into the back of her head, and her face goes from red to pink to pale. "Mia! Are you okay?" I ask, but before she can answer, white clabbered milk begins to pour from her open mouth. "Mia!" I try to stay focused on the road, but the look on her face is so pitiful and scared, I can't continue to drive.

I pull the truck over and stop on a hill on the interstate. I put the gearshift in neutral and look over the seat to see her mouth open again, and a new fountain of white erupts. "Mommy!" she sobs. What is happening? I flip through every possible scenario I can imagine from seizures to cardiac arrest. Her mouth opens one last time to allow what is left in her tiny stomach to escape.

She shakes and spits pieces of spoiled milk from her wet lips. "Mommy!" she continues to scream. It takes a moment for the shock to leave me, and I slowly begin to realize that she has just vomited for the first time.

My heart aches for her as my body remembers and conjures the familiar sour wetness in my mouth. I instantly think of a queasy stomach. Of burning acid moving through my throat. Of shaking with chills. Of the horrible taste left behind. All I can think of is holding my sweet baby who is now covered in this morning's milk. Her black shirt is now gray, and her pants are soaked. She holds out her arms to me, and I jump from the truck, run around the front, and try to open her door.

But the handle moves. When I try to pull it again, the hard black plastic flips out of my hand, and I watch in horror as the truck begins to roll backwards down the hill. It moves slowly at first, but it begins to pick up momentum as an eighteen-wheeler pushes up the hill behind us.

Panic fills me. I run after the truck and try to pull it to a stop. The shiny green enamel slips from my sweaty fingers, and I fight the urge to scream as my adrenaline begins to take over. I catch up to the truck, pull the passenger door open, and dive into the seat. The door swings closed onto my dangling legs as I lean across the console, searching frantically for the brake pedal. When my hands finally find the hard rubber, I push it with all my might. The truck comes to a hard stop, and both kids cry out at the sudden lurch of the truck.

I slam my left hand onto the emergency brake and look to the light on the dash to make sure it is on. The red letters stare back at me. I sit up in the passenger seat, and the truck shakes as the eighteen-wheeler roars past us. Behind us, there are no more cars for miles. We are still on the side of the interstate, and our truck has only moved a few feet, but it feels as though we have crossed miles of dangerous territory.

"Mommy!" Amelia screams again from the backseat. I try to settle my stomach, but the realization that I could have just watched my children be destroyed by a truck is overwhelming. I see myself falling under the truck as I try to catch it, and my sweet babies rolling away to a violent explosion. I see my hands searching for the brake and not finding it before I am ejected from the vehicle and they are left alone in a horrific crash. I feel my sweaty hands missing the brake pedal over and over again, and I jump out of the truck and vomit on the side of the interstate.

"Mommy!" she cries again from behind the truck window. I turn to her, wipe my mouth clean, and open her door. "It is okay, baby. Mommy is right here," I tell her as I pull her beautiful curls from the white, sticky mess on her shirt. "You just threw up. I'm going to take care of you," I say as I attempt to clean her and calm her

I try to calm myself as well. "I'm going to take you somewhere so that I can change your clothes," I say, stroking her soft face. Her cries subside. I hand her dolly to her. "Mommy! I got dolly mess too!" Her body begins to shake in new violent sobs. She holds her special baby out to me and says, "Clean, Mommy! I mess dolly!" She is pitiful, and my heart aches. Her need replaces my anger and fear, and I search for something, anything to clean dolly's cloth face. I pull one of David's truck-cleaning rags from the floorboard and scrub dolly until there is no trace of white on her pink, plush face.

When Amelia is quiet and no longer shaking, I settle back into the driver's seat. I call my mother and ask her for advice. I tell her nothing of my horrific lapse of judgment. I don't want to scare her. I have terrified myself. She tells me to call my father who is just miles away from me, visiting with friends at the quaint London, Kentucky, airport. When he answers the phone, I can feel myself beginning to relax.

"Dad, Amelia just threw up everywhere. Can I stop by there and have you watch Elijah while I clean her?" I beg. When his composed answer flows through the phone, I find the strength to start driving again. I take the London exit, and move toward some sense of sanity. "We are almost there, baby. Just a few more minutes," I tell her. She says nothing. Her cries have eased to a whimper, and she looks out the window at the passing trees.

When we arrive at the small, familiar airport, my father and his friend greet me at the door. I walk to the back of the truck, rummage through the diaper bag for her clean clothes, and move around the back of the truck to get her. But my father is already there, pulling her from her seat. He cuddles her in his arms, takes the clothes from my hand, and whisks her into the airport entrance. I follow him with Elijah's carrier. When Elijah is settled just inside the door, I unbuckle her car seat, take it inside, and begin to clean it. Amelia's excited voice bounces from wall to wall in the bathroom.

I work frantically on her car seat until there is little evidence of her explosion. Her voice moves from the bathroom to the hallway, and she is, once again, in my father's arms. She is smiling and seems completely relaxed and happy. "Thank you so much, Dad. She was so pitiful. I didn't know what to do," I tell him. I don't mention forgetting the emergency brake or the need to dive back into the truck to set it. Just thinking of it again causes my stomach to churn, and I feel the blood leave my face. It was stupid, and I am ashamed that I panicked and made such an obvious mistake.

With Amelia content and in dry clothes, I load the truck again and set out once more for Louisville. I don't want to disappoint David's family. Or David. Amelia and I both wave to my father. He waves in return and walks back into the airport.

I pull away still chastising myself. I try to push the incident from my mind and give driving my complete devotion. All is well for miles. As we near Louisville, the tension in my head begins to clear. The end is in sight.

"Mommy!" Amelia screams from the backseat. I know that scream now and realize what it means. I look into the rearview mirror to find her spitting as her mouth waters and the color drains from her face again. When her eyes begin to roll into the back of her head, I try to soothe her with my voice. I search the road for the next exit sign. It is ten miles away. "It's okay, baby. You are going to be fine," I chant to her. But everything is not fine. She explodes. Again. And then screams at the top of her lungs. Again.

Elijah wakes from his blissful sleep, wailing. My head pounds. The next exit finally comes into sight, and I leave the interstate. Amelia screams. Elijah cries.

I pull into a gas station and attempt to clean her again. I have no more fresh clothes with me. I didn't plan well enough. She is wet and shaking. She reaches for me again, and I hold her and stroke her hair. I am covered with her vomit, standing in a gas station on Thanksgiving. I miss David.

I call his parents to tell them I am nearly there, and that Amelia and I will be coming in with vomit all over us. They are kind and concerned. They tell me to take my time and that they will have a warm bath waiting for her. I fight the urge to cry as I end the call.

I try to clean Amelia's seat as much as possible. There are only a few wipes left. Elijah is hungry, Amelia is wet and shaking, and it is only getting colder outside. We snuggle one last time, and then I buckle her back into her filthy car seat. I feel like a horrible mother.

She cries to get out of her seat. Elijah cries to escape his. I force myself not to cry because I can't allow for another costly mistake while driving. "We are almost to Mimi and Poppy's house, babies. Just hang on," I tell them in the mirror. Amelia meets my eyes with tears, and I want nothing more than to hold her.

When we finally turn onto the familiar road of their house, I can feel myself beginning to exhale. They meet us on the stairs, and David's father helps me remove Amelia and her car seat from the truck. "Go to Mimi, baby. She will help you," I tell her and begin to pull her car seat apart once again.

I feed Elijah, settle his tiny belly, and then pull the fabric and buckles from the car seat. Elijah squirms next to me on the carpet, playing with his feet in the air. Amelia splashes and laughs from the bathroom, and I wonder what could have caused her violent explosions. She has no fever. No symptoms at all.

When she is bathed, dried, and spoiled, she begins to settle into bed for a nap. Elijah is already sleeping. I close the door to her room and leave her to her clean dolly and her books. She is content and exhausted. I pace the floor, talking to David's family and praying that he will call soon. I don't tell them anything about chasing our truck. I can't. I can hardly face what I did on my own.

I need to hear his voice, his calming, velvet voice so that I can find my center again. It seems like hours before my cell phone rings with the familiar Fort Drum operator's number connecting me to Iraq. When I answer, the tears are already pouring even before I hear his delayed "Hello." I don't say anything, only cry. "What's wrong, baby? Are you okay?" he asks with concern.

I don't want to worry him or tell him what I did. I don't want to explain that I am a horrible mother and that he can't even trust me to drive his children anywhere. I convulse with tears and shake violently. I know that I need to tell him. We promised no secrets. No matter what they might be.

"I have something to tell you. First, let me say that I am so sorry," I begin. He is quiet. He has learned to listen more than talk with only ten minutes and constant delays. "Amelia threw up in the truck while I was driving, and I panicked," I blurt. "Is she okay?" he asks after the delay, softly adding, "Just calm down and talk to me."

"I pulled over to the side of the interstate to help her, and I didn't set the brake," I begin. My stomach churns. I feel the need to vomit again. "The truck started moving, and I was on a hill. I caught up with it and opened the door," I explain. But there is no explanation for my stupidity. There is no reason I can give for putting our babies at risk.

"I jumped in and put on the brake. We only moved a few feet, but we could have rolled onto the interstate. I could have killed us!" I sob into the phone. "Calm down," he whispers, "breathe and calm down." I listen, steady my breathing, and prepare myself for him to attack. I wait for him to scream that I should have my babies stripped from me. I expect him to show me no mercy. I don't blame him. It is what I would do.

"David, I'm so sorry," I say. He is quiet. "Don't apologize to me," he says. His calmness stops me. "You didn't do anything wrong," he explains. I yell, "What do you mean? I did everything wrong! I could have waited until the next exit! I could have not panicked! I could have set the brake like a normal person! How can you say that?"

"I can say that because I'm not perfect, either. You made a mistake. You fixed it," he calmly explains. "But that mistake could have taken our babies," I cry. "Don't look at what could have happened. Look at what did. You moved. You stopped it. And now, you are safe and getting ready to eat turkey," he says. I stop short. I have forgotten that it is Thanksgiving.

"David, I'm so sorry. Happy Thanksgiving," I finally say. I hear him laugh as he echoes the sentiment. He says, "I'll be able to call you again today. Don't worry about wrapping it all up in ten minutes. Do me a favor, will ya? When it's time to say what we are thankful for this year, tell my family that I am thankful for a wife that always lands on her feet. Okay?" I cry, "David, I'm so ashamed of myself. I just totally screwed up." He replies, "Well, I'm not ashamed of you. I am more proud of you today than I ever have been." His voice breaks. "Thanks for telling me. That took guts."

"I doubt I have the guts to tell anyone else," I whisper, "but today I'm thankful for saying 'I do.'" There is a long pause between us and the unspoken words are filled with emotion and devotion. "I'll call back and chat with the fam," he says before the call ends.

And he does. He calls us on the computer's web cam and chats, and laughs, and pretends that our previous conversation never happened. And I am thankful for that.

Looking to Baghdad

Today is the day of the Iraqi elections, and David is there. He is in the middle of it with the people whom this war is supposedly for. There is nonstop television coverage of the election, and I look for him. When he first told me that he wouldn't be able to call for a few days, I was upset. He didn't tell me why. He couldn't. "Just tell me if you are going to be in danger," I begged him. "I can't answer that. I can't tell you any details. You have to stop asking," he pleaded. "I just hate it when I don't hear from you. It makes me scared," I told him. "I will call when I can. Kiss the babies. I love you," he'd said just before the satellite call disconnected and his voice left the receiver.

It made me crazy not to know any details about his mission. But now, as the election unfolds, it is obvious why he couldn't tell me where he would be. For a change, I actually turn on the news and watch it. There is excitement in the air. There are smiles on faces. But images of positioned soldiers as well as bulletproofed reporters tell of the danger surrounding the elections.

It is thrilling to know that he is there. And terrifying at the same time. I am worried that something will happen. That insurgents will attack and David will be wounded. I am scared that I may actually see it happen. I try to turn away, to not watch the constant streaming news coverage. But that is impossible. I search the crowd, hoping to catch a glimpse of him. I scour the screen for just a glance of his boots, his back, his helmet, his gun, or some flicker of his emotions. I wish I could be there with him. He is now part of history.

So many questions crowd my mind. I want to know how he feels and what he is thinking. Is this why he joined? Is this his calling? Is this what propels him? Is this what makes it tolerable to be away from his family? Is it this kind of change, this kind of elation on people's faces?

We wait all day to hear from him. When he finally calls, the connection is bad. There is always a delay in the conversation. But today the delay is long and full of static. After a few attempts to talk on the phone, he finally resorts to the computer.

I hear the buzz of the instant messenger and run from the living room into my parents' computer room. I pull out the chair and begin typing to him. He calls us on the computer. We can see him on the web cam, but he has no microphone. My parents have a microphone and no web cam. It is an odd conversation of us shouting questions, seeing the delayed reaction on his face, and then watching him type the answers.

I ask him endless questions about the election. "So was your mission today to work the elections? Were you there?" He answers none of them. He only says that he had a fun day, but it was no big deal. All he wants to hear about is the kids. He wants to know what they have done today without him.

There is a glimmer of his thoughts about it all when he sends pictures in his e-mail. He sends one of a small girl. Her father lovingly holds her and smiles. He holds her purple finger up to David's camera. She had dipped her finger in ink to be a part of the experience. The women in his pictures are covered from head to toe. They are voting. There are elated men. They are voting.

I hold Amelia and Elijah on my lap and scroll through David's pictures. Amelia asks questions nonstop as we look from image to image. "What Daddy doing? That Daddy? Where Daddy?" I point to him on the screen, and show Elijah too. Amelia stops when she sees the little girl. "That girl with Daddy?" I look into the screen and stare as familiar brown eyes, brimming with life and energy, stare into my own. She is a world away from us, but she has the same zest, the same need as my little girl. I know David sees his children in her face, too. I am positive that her face is part of what drives and propels him through his days.

"Yeah, Daddy is with that little girl. He is trying to keep her happy," I tell her. In my mind, I can see hundreds of pictures of David holding Amelia. They are both smiling, looking straight into the camera. This child looks happy and momentarily carefree. David helped do that. In some small way, Amelia, Elijah, and I helped, too.

A Welcome Distraction

People tell me to focus on the joys of the holidays and the time with my parents. I try. Instead, my mind scrolls through memories of holidays spent as a family. Images of the two of us sledding in snow engulf me. I hear his laughter. Thoughts of him cutting his very first Christmas tree invade my mind. He drags it down the mountain behind him, puffing on a cheap cigar and talking about the adrenaline rushing through his veins from his "first kill." I reflect on the soft candlelight of our first lit menorah as a married couple and remember the winter snow falling softly and quietly as we slept in the hospital bed with our new baby.

December is a special month for us. It holds birthdays, Hanukkah, Christmas, and New Year's Eve. It holds everything us. The most important December event for us, however, is the annual basketball game between our rival teams. Nothing compares to the heated games and the passionate rivalry that cooks between us.

David and I are huge college basketball fans. I love the University of Kentucky, and David loves his hometown team, the

University of Louisville. They are both Kentucky teams, and they play each other every December. David and I always paint our faces, wear our respective colors, and trash-talk the other's team. Nothing gets in the way of our favorite game of the year. Not even when David's red and black face paint caused mayhem when we both sat in UK's blue and white student section at the annual game. Not even when we persuaded the doctor to release me from the hospital a day early after Amelia was born so that we could catch the game from our own couch. We have always been dedicated to our colors, and we let little stand in the way of this special game.

We're not unusual. Nearly the entire state of Kentucky stops for the UK–U of L basketball game. In Lexington, fire hydrants are painted blue to support the Cats. In Louisville, cardinals are painted everywhere. UK's Kentucky TeleCare Network and the Freedom Calls Foundation understand that Kentucky stops for this moment, and they are allowing Kentucky fans in Iraq to do the same. Because of their generosity, willingness, and their volunteer efforts to connect families at home to loved ones in Iraq, David and I will once again watch the game together at a massive teleconference being held at Rupp Arena. Thousands of family members will see their soldiers and marines, and I will finally be able to hear and see David laughing and talking without delays or dropped connections. I feel hopeful, joyful anticipation for the first time since he left.

I wake Amelia and tell her today she is going to see her daddy on a big television screen. She digs her tiny fists into her eyes and curls her legs into her chest, then pushes them, stretching and squirming. "Mia, honey, we need to get ready. Today is 'Go Cats' with Daddy," I tell her as I pull her to my chest and stroke her curls. She cuddles with me for a moment until she realizes what I have told her. She jumps from the bed and runs into the living room. "Go Cats!" she screams.

We are all festive and excited. My mom and I dress in blue. We put Amelia in a new blue and white cheerleader outfit. I want to make sure that we are slathered in my team's colors. This year's game will be no different than any other. In his heart, although he

40

will be in uniform, David will be bursting with red and black pride. And I won't disappoint him by not wearing blue.

Even Elijah wears blue. I have no doubt David's family will not allow him to remain blue, but I attempt to sneak his blue clothes past them. I spend nearly an hour getting dressed and ready. This will be the first time he has seen me, in full, since he left. I take a few minutes to put the finishing touches on my face: foundation, mascara, and eyeliner. Although he prefers no makeup, I want to be beautiful for him. And I want to make him smile. On my cheek, I paint my team's letters, UK, in blue and white. I know he will be looking for it.

My mother, my two babies, and I load into the truck to go see him. It is a beautiful December day. We drive the familiar route to Lexington and excitement and anticipation fill the truck. "We see Daddy today?" Amelia asks from her seat. I look at her in the rear-view mirror. She wouldn't allow me to paint her cheek, but the blue and white bows in her hair bring a smile to my face. "Yeah, we are going to see Daddy. What are you going to tell him, baby?" I prod her. "Go Cats!" she squeals as she shakes her blue pom-poms in the air.

We meet with David's family in Lexington. His parents, sister, and grandpa all tumble out of the car, dressed in red and black. In David's mother's hands she holds a tiny bundle of red. "He's already dressed," I tell her. "No need to taint him with red." I laugh as I try to keep her from the door. She pushes me aside and pulls Elijah from the truck. She puts a tiny cardinal outfit on my once-blue baby. We are truly a family divided. David would have it no other way.

Rupp Arena vibrates with excitement. The game is secondary today. So many families are there for their marines and soldiers. "My marine bleeds blue," says one shirt. "My captain is a cardinal," reads another. Red, black, white, and blue are mixed with images of uniforms, camouflage, and yellow ribbons. Everyone is smiling. This will be the first time in months that many have set eyes on their marine or soldier. There is no thought of war today. There is only the promise of forgetting it.

We walk through the crowd of families searching for the teleconference room. A news team stops us, struck by our stark divisions, and asks if we mind giving an interview. "Not at all," I say. The reporter gives an introduction to the camera and sets up the circumstances. "Who are you here for today?" she asks.

We all stammer, "My husband," "My son-in-law," "My grandson," "My son," "My brother." "And who will he be rooting for today?" the reporter asks. "Unfortunately, U of L," I say with a smirk. I don't hear the rest of the interview. She speaks to my mother and to David's family while I hold Amelia in my arms and stare at Elijah. The moment feels surreal, and I become lost in a world somewhere between the buzzing arena and a memory, or a dream of things to come. David is in red, holding Elijah in blue, and Amelia has a red cheerleader outfit competing with the blue of my shirt. We are walking, laughing. We are older. Happier.

My mother nudges me to bring me back to the interview. The reporter gives the final details of the game and teleconference, and I shake her hand in thanks as they begin to pack their equipment. We walk away feeling famous. "You think our swollen heads will fit in the teleconference room?" I ask and laugh as I link my arm through my mother's.

The teleconference waiting area is filled with signs, with hats, and with soldiers' faces on the fronts of shirts. We're the first on the list. As I enter, with the others on my heels, I see David on the big television screen. He is anxious, excited, fidgeting, and he is trying to be patient.

He looks beautiful. Elated. "Hey family!" he calls to us with tears in the corner of his eye. He waves and moves his chair closer to the camera. His face comes into full view.

It is two in the morning there. He had to take a long helicopter ride to another camp just to see us. He's tired, but he doesn't show it. Only pure excitement to see our faces is visible.

"I see at least some of you have a sense of the better team," he says with an impish grin. I am so thankful that our initial greeting isn't filled with tears. It isn't filled with emotional conversation and questions about his safety. I can't focus on that today. I only want to hear predictions about the game. I only want him to make fun of me. I want him to laugh at my face paint. "I know. I tried to give your parents some blue, but they insisted on the losing colors," I shoot back at him. His wide grin shows the beautiful space in his teeth that I love so much.

We gather around the table and begin to talk to him. I hear the others' voices, but I can only stare. I can only see him. I am engulfed by his enormous smile. He looks happy, content, as if for a moment he's unaware of the war surrounding him. His eyes follow Amelia around the room. She shows him her new shoes. She talks about his face. He watches her with tears in his eyes and joy in his heart. He laughs at her pom-poms and cringes when she cheers, "Go Cats!" "Who taught her that kind of language?" he asks. His eyes twinkle with delight.

David's sister holds Elijah up to the screen, and David is amazed at how much his baby has changed. He asks if Elijah is heavy and if he is sleeping. His sister moves Elijah closer to the screen. He is breathing deeply and David watches him, fascinated. "He's huge!" he says. "I can't believe how much he has changed."

I am thankful to see him smiling. It is a day that will stand out for the both of us for the rest of our lives. We have been here so many times before. We have been in the stands, under the stands, and behind the stands cheering our teams. We have painted our faces and we have screamed until we had no voices. But this time feels weighted. It feels exponentially different.

I begin to allow my mind to wander into the "what if" section of the arena. What if this is our last game? What if something happens? I have to check myself before I allow my fear to ruin this day of peace. It is a day of escape. I choose to pretend that we are sitting next to each other trading insults, laughing, and cheering. If I push it all from my mind, maybe it will cease to exist.

I hear him say my name, and I turn to meet his gaze. He tells me that I am beautiful and that I look wonderful. He hasn't seen me since I began my transformation from post-delivery mom. I love that he has noticed the gradual change. He watches me with the children and tells me that I am such a wonderful mother. His voice doesn't break, but I can hear where it would if he let it. I can see the reality in his heart.

He continues to compliment me until I turn my cheek to the monitor. His radiant smile disappears into a frown. His pulls his eyebrows together and crosses his arms across his chest. I am confused at first, but his sneaking grin defies his fake anger. I know that look. I walk closer to the television and push my face toward the screen.

"What is that horrible thing on your face?" He laughs. I knew he would love it. This deployment will not take away our joy or our ability to laugh at and with each other. I stare at him. "Don't be jealous because you don't have one," I say with a wink. "Oh, don't worry. I wouldn't dare trash my face with those colors," he says.

I take my seat again and quietly listen as he talks to my mother and his family. He talks and laughs and smiles and listens. He trades stories with his World War II veteran grandfather, and he laughs when Amelia's head wanders into the camera's view, taking up the entire screen. He plays peek-a-boo with her as she giggles and stares. He is jovial. I know of his hardship, of his pain, and of his weariness. But there are no signs of it today.

We talk and laugh with him until someone enters the room to say the governor of Kentucky would like to speak with David. I see him sit tall and feel proud, and I marvel at the man that he has become. I am mystified by the stature he holds.

The door to the teleconference room opens, and we all fidget when the governor enters. He takes the time to introduce himself, take pictures with Amelia and Elijah, and to thank us for our service at home before he sits at the table to talk to David. David speaks with the governor, and he listens while he is thanked and congratulated and consoled. He describes the Iraqi elections. He talks about the state of Iraq. He discusses little of his sacrifice, and he praises his fellow soldiers for enduring such long and painful deployments. He accepts the appreciation of the governor, and he respectfully disagrees when the governor predicts that UK will win today's game. "I'm sorry, sir. You are wrong. I just can't say that the Cats could ever beat the Cards," he says. The governor laughs, takes more pictures, and politely leaves the room to go visit with other families.

We talk and laugh and listen for forty-five minutes. I don't want to leave him. I don't want to leave the room. I have a moment alone with him and can no longer hold it in. He talks softly to me while the rest of the family leaves us alone. He whispers to me that he loves me, that he is proud of me, and that I am everything that he needs me to be. I try not to cry. I try not to miss him. I try to focus on him being here with me today. I try to be thankful for that.

"Don't cry, babe. You will mess up your face paint." I look at him and smile. I giggle and then explode with laughter. "There. That's better," he says. "I would tell you to use a handkerchief, but it is hard when you don't have one." Fresh tears roll down my cheeks as he reaches into a pocket on his uniform. He pulls the yellow fabric to his face. "It smells like you. Thanks for giving it to me."

I bite my bottom lip and smile. "I wasn't sure if you would like it," I say. He smiles and says, "I carry it with me every second of the day." He looks into my eyes for what seems like hours. We say nothing.

A woman enters the room to tell us that other soldiers are on the phone waiting for their families. She turns to David to tell him that time is up, but they want David to stay on the line long enough to be on the big screen in Rupp Arena. Each family will stand on the court before the game, listening to the governor speak to the soldiers in Iraq. David, along with a few other soldiers, will have the opportunity to address the entire arena. This is what we have waited for: David and I will have the chance to represent our teams for the whole arena.

We parade onto the court through the sound of thunder from the arena's applause. David and several other men and women in uniform are on the screen, hungrily peering at this window into home.

The National Anthem sends my whole body into shakes. Tears wet my face. The entire arena is looking at these men and women who in turn can see their families. The governor takes center court and speaks about courage, bravery, and sacrifice. He asks if the soldiers have anything to say. I see David's face come into full view.

I hold my breath, entirely expecting him to launch into a sweet serenade of how much his family means to him.

"I just want to say hello to my wife and kids. And I would like to say that U of L is going to win!" The entire arena begins to shake with a dull echo of boos.

The camera turns to me to capture my reaction, and my face fills the jumbo screen. All I can think of is every game David and I have watched together. I feel every laugh we've shared, every joyous moment. I remember freezing together outside this arena, huddled in a blanket as we awaited our chance to enter. I remember watching from the television in his tiny apartment, our faces painted, still. I remember every game and every moment of blue and white and red and black with him.

I boo him, too.

The soldier next to him grabs him in a headlock and sings the praises of UK. The entire arena erupts in applause. It isn't what many would expect. It isn't focused on family. But it is exactly what David and I need. It is a taste of each other. It is a glimpse of us.

The families are escorted off the arena floor, and David's family leaves the court to return to the viewing and refreshment area. Elijah is with them, sleeping in his red clothes. But Amelia, my mother, and I linger on the court, begging the officials and the escorts to allow us to see the players come out. With the promise to leave as soon as the players enter, we are allowed to stay behind. There are fireworks. There is a light show. We jump up and down, screaming for our team. I hold Amelia in her UK outfit, and she shakes her pom-poms and cheers "Go Cats" along with the crowd. I smile freely, without the habitual lapse into a frown that has interrupted my smiles for these weeks. I laugh and cheer and bounce my daughter to the sound of the band.

After the game, with my face paint streaked by tears and my arms full of sleeping babies, I leave the arena feeling proud, hyper, and thankful that David and I didn't have to miss the game this year. My mother, my children, and I pile into the truck, weary from the excitement, and turn on the radio to listen to the post-game commentary. The announcer talks about the soldiers and the families on the court. He discusses the game, the governor, and the one soldier who caused an entire arena to shake with boos.

I laugh. "David would be so pleased," I say to my mother. She grins in agreement, and we leave the arena with snapshot memories of blue streamers, news interviews, fireworks, a roaring crowd, and David's vibrant smile on the big screen.

My joy is still with me the next day. My father has been up for hours collecting papers. I look through the headlines. They are covered with pictures of blue, white, red, black, and camouflage. Just seeing them brings an instant smile to my face. My picture is on the Internet news. The photographer caught me just as I booed David Amelia is in my arms wearing blue and white. David's mother stands next to me, in red and black, holding Elijah in his U of L clothes. I can see in the picture our determination not to allow this deployment to eat us. I can see games past and games in the future.

I e-mail the picture to David. He's still filled with excitement from seeing us and watching the game. I know that he went to bed smiling that night. Even though UK won the game.

Masquerade

Today is my birthday. Tomorrow is Christmas. The next day is Amelia's second birthday. It is Hanukkah. Next week is New Year's Eve.

I need to lie to my children and craft a deliberate strand of half-truths in order for them to enjoy their holidays. I need to lie to them with smiles, with cheerfulness, with laughter.

I need to search my body and mind and dig deep from within to make them believe I am fulfilled and I am excited about all that the holidays represent: family, tradition, and togetherness. Everything that we, at this moment, are not.

I pretend I'm not focused on David and attempt excitement about gifts and about watching the children open them. I want to be excited, to care about presents and food and caroling, but it all feels jaded and pointless. He should be here to enjoy their faces. He should be here to hold them as they light the menorah. He should be here to share my cake. He should be here to watch Amelia blow out her candles. He should be here to make and break resolutions. He should be here.

I smile on my birthday and push through the day, trying not to focus on everything he would say to me were he here, or the laughs we'd share over the number of candles on my cake. I close my eyes and try not to imagine his sweet kiss waking me from pleasant dreams. "Happy birthday, baby," he says somewhere in the cobwebs of my mind.

I open my gifts; what is given passes me by, lost in the paper. Who is talking to me? What is being said? I smile. And nod. And laugh.

In bed, on my birthday, I am alone and completely lonely. In my parents' house. Nearly every birthday of my life has been celebrated here. Why doesn't that bring me comfort or soften the blow of his absence?

I try to fall asleep, but I keep thinking of him. Of our earlier conversation, of his strained jokes about my age, of him trying to persevere through this. We're both trying to avoid the fact that he's not here. I think and think and think of him until I am buried in misery. I try to sleep, to relax. His face behind my eyes will not allow it. Broken sleep finally comes, but it is filled with images of him smashing cake in my face and kissing me goodbye.

Waking from the barest of rests to Christmas morning feels unreal. My niece and nephew play with their new toys. They happily chatter as they proudly display each new treasure. Their sweet smiles and vibrant red hair are intoxicating, and I want to lose myself in their excitement. I want my brother's contagious gift-giving spirit to engulf me, and I desperately want not to disappoint my sister-in-law. She bites her lip with anticipation as I open the gift she thoughtfully picked out for me. I hug her and thank her for being her. Their love is thick and overflowing, but my heart still won't lift along with their joy. Only his misery consumes me.

I turn to my babies and hope their excitement will dull the constant ache in my chest. Amelia begins to fully realize that these new gifts are for her, and she begins to tear into the paper. She bursts with excitement, and she looks to me for more. "Look my presents, Mommy!"

I lie to my daughter and tell her that I am so happy, that this is such a fun day. It is a day to celebrate family, peace, and fulfillment. She laughs and plays and is momentarily unaware that David isn't here. She is a child again. She doesn't have a burden on her shoulders. She is a normal toddler playing with her Christmas toys. I want to freeze that moment for her. To hold it, captivate it, and produce it again for her on a day when she aches and cries for him.

Elijah is in my arms bouncing to the rhythm of Christmas music. Then my mother holds him in the air and sings to him. He smiles in return. The love and concern my family has for us are abundant and plentiful. They all look at me with knowing eyes, and to their credit, show me no pity. They show no recognition of his absence. And I love them for that. Not talking about it is the only thing that keeps me composed.

I open my gifts with a complete desire to be present and involved. I want to be here with my family, enjoying all that they offer, but I can't stop thinking of him. Is he on a mission? Is he in danger? Is someone with him? Is he lonely? Is he missing us? Are they celebrating over there? Are they working? Does he have enough of home to keep him company?

When he does call, a hush falls over the room as my family listens intently for any hint of his demeanor. He saturates all of our thoughts. Even my niece and nephew stiffen when they realize Uncle David is on the phone.

For ten short minutes we talk about gifts. He talks about what he got and about what others got. He doesn't talk about his mission or his Christmas dinner in the chow hall. He talks about lighting the menorah every night. He talks about wanting to eat applesauce and latkes and about wanting to play with Amelia and her new toys. He is aching to hold Elijah and to watch him stare with amazement at the glowing candles and twinkling Christmas lights.

We don't talk about the pain of the holidays. We don't discuss the strain in our voices or the tears that we are both holding back. We speak nothing of what we are missing of each other.

Melissa Seligman

★ ★ ★

Two special days down. Now my energy is on Amelia's birthday. I pause just before entering her room. I have to be excited, explosive. She deserves that from her mother. She is two, and Daddy isn't here. Her eyes gleam when I say, "Good morning, birthday girl!"

She runs through my parents' house and jumps into my father's arms. Hugs and kisses and cheers from my mother and father greet her. Family members and friends come to her party and praise her for being such a big girl. Affection showers her today. I beg God to let that be enough, to help me believe it is enough.

My two-year-old daughter blows out her candles and tears through her gifts. She squeals with each new treasure, and then laughs, plays, hugs, and kisses. I hold her longer and kiss her harder and tell her of her birth. She is interested only for a moment about the story of the first time I held her and the first time David kissed her. I want to tell her about the words he said. As he sat next to me, he held her so tenderly. "I was put on this earth to be your husband and her father," he'd said. It was the first moment that my heart expanded. She is too busy enjoying her birthday to hear my memories of her.

David has a calling card today, so we get a chance to talk longer. But there is only silence on the other end while he listens to her party, to the laughter, to the songs, and to the happiness that he can only imagine.

"Today is a pretty rough day," he says. "I can't imagine, David," I reply. I don't know what to say to him. I sit and listen to his silence. Amelia comes to the phone to talk to him. She has been running, and she is hot and sweaty.

"It's my birthday, Daddy! I got presents. Love you. Bye." She is off and running again. Quietly, he sobs. "This is the hardest thing I have ever done," he says. "I can't imagine," I repeat softly.

His pain stays with me for the rest of the day as I try to keep from imagining him, alone in his room, holding the pink dolly that he took with him from her bed. It is painful to think of him weeping and mourning his absence at her party. But it is this image that

51

keeps me so deeply in love with him. To think of his suffering makes my chest feel tight and heavy, but his chest must feel cracked, raw, and exposed.

I put her to bed with new stuffed animals and dreams of cake and ice cream. I sing softly to her and linger for a few moments longer, taking the time to reflect on the two years she has blessed me. She looks bigger today. But her soft, delicate face still resembles the sleeping cherub of yesterday.

I close her door behind me and settle into bed next to Elijah's cradle. He softly breathes and sighs, and I try to push David's tears from my mind and attempt to prepare myself for tomorrow's celebration.

After breakfast with my parents, the kids settle in the truck as we again prepare for the drive to Louisville. I try to push thoughts of past Hanukkahs from my mind. I try not to think of our first Hanukkah together or the glow of the candles. Instead, I drive with determination and preparation. My ability to function will not be destroyed because I can't stop missing him.

When we finally reach their house, Amelia runs through the door, screaming, "Mimi, Poppy!" There are menorahs everywhere, and she is in love with them. She can't wait to light the candles. Elijah comes alive as he begins to realize that we are in a new place and that different people are holding him and cooing at him. His beautiful eyes begin to sparkle as he notices the sun catching the stained glass in the window.

I pretend I'm excited about the gifts waiting for them and squeal with Amelia before telling her that we have to talk to Daddy on the computer before we open them. She doesn't protest. She has adjusted to life with him on a screen. Sometimes we can hear him now. Sometimes we can't. We spend our days waiting to hear him signal us on the computer. The timing is random. The conversation is often delayed, full of static, and lasts only thirty minutes at a time. But at least we can see him. He is still part of us this way.

I try not to think about being with David's family without him. Pictures of him throughout his childhood surround me. I try not to look at his father and not to see his face in his father's face or his hair in his father's hair. I want to hug his father longer just because he looks like David. Amelia, too, registers the resemblance. She stares at David's father. She walks after him and touches his leg. She searches his face for anything that looks like David.

I try not to look at David's grandfather and at what he will become in our old age. Somewhere in my mind, we are together, older and holding our grandchildren. I imagine holding his hand while we gather around the menorah, watching the glow of the lit candles dancing in our future grandchildren's eyes. I believe it will happen, but I have to stop thinking about it to get through this day.

David's eyes, hair, and profile all come alive for me in my nephew. His eyes reflect the childhood I can only imagine David having. In my mind, David runs and plays with his sisters just as Amelia runs and plays with her cousins, now. The pain in my mother-in-law's face is unmistakable as she watches her absent son's children. My father-in-law hides the tears that could freely flow. Worry betrays his sister's voice when she asks how David is doing. The joy of seeing him at the UK–U of L game is quickly fleeting. Even his smiling face on the screen can't erase their sadness of his absence today.

His name floats through the house on everyone's lips. I try not to cry as person after person comes into the computer room to see his face on the screen. I try not to want to stay on the computer with him all day or to see the look on his face and the pain in his eyes that he isn't here with his family. Sadness is in his voice. He wants so badly to be here to celebrate and eat latkes and applesauce.

I try not to hear the excitement coming from the other room as I stare into his face; his lonely, broken, and courageous face. It is the face that he allows only me to see. And I see it so completely.

Amelia tears through paper again and through the gifts. She becomes more and more excited with each new thing.

We gather around the tables to eat latkes and applesauce. Amelia pushes them into her mouth and barely swallows the last bite before asking for more. She reminds me so much of him. Her face. Her hair. Her actions. I fill her plate again and smile as she plays with the dreidels on the table.

As we drive off, I try not to concentrate on his face on the screen and his heartbreak at not being there. I try not to think of all that is surrounding us and all that is going on without us. I recognize this feeling of standing still while the world flies past me. I felt it on my first ride on a carousel. My father took me. I tried to stay calm while I rode it all by myself. The horse moved gracefully and beautifully, while the outside laughter and noise became distorted and terrifying. I searched for my father in the crowd, but only saw blurs of light and heard faceless voices cheering.

Those same feelings of methodical chaos engulf me now. We have become a sideshow. We are in our own amusement park. We are frozen in time, waiting for life to begin again.

I try to play with the kids, to laugh with them as we spin round and round on our own little ride. I try to dismiss the crowd that has gathered to watch, to laugh, to hug, and to support. They are all peripheral. They are faceless and plentiful. I try to thank them, to rely on and trust them. But the ride spins out of control. Each face becomes more and more blurry and distorted as the carousel becomes unmanageable.

I reach for the nearest horse as my children scream with joy. They are oblivious to the fear that is bubbling inside of me. We are on this ride alone. We are in the middle, watching from the inside while life goes on around us. There is no end in sight.

I look at my babies' faces and know that I have to make them believe that I am okay, that David is okay, and that we are still a united family. My children deserve at least that, my lies. I cling to my babies as I give in to the momentum, ride the carousel with them, and save a seat for David.

Unraveling

We have been in Kentucky for several weeks, and the emotional strain is beginning to wear on Amelia. Her daddy left. I took her from her home and brought her here. None of her toys are here. She is hurting. She is reeling. She is confused and rattled. I am blind to this. I float from person to person as they all tell me how strong I am and how strong David is. Friends and family tell me how great it is for me to be here instead of alone in New York. I try to believe them and focus on pulling myself up by the bootstraps. All the while, my parents nurse me through it all. In the meantime, Amelia is here now, trying to figure it all out on her own.

How can I possibly expect her to understand? To realize that I need time to adjust, time to mourn, time to miss him, and time to get my bearings? I need her to give the time and the understanding of my pain all to me. I expect too much.

When she finally begins to scream her protests out loud, I decide she is terribly two. When she tells me, "No. Don't want to," I think she is asserting her independence. I overlook the obvious problem and avoid dealing with it by blaming outside factors such as age or developmental stages.

One day she finally breaks me out of my stupidity. My father tickles and giggles with Elijah while I watch, oblivious to Amelia's warning signs. My eyes are focused on the joy in Elijah's laugh. Hearing it allows me to avoid the reality hovering and threatening to fall into my lap. Amelia defiantly throws her toys across my parents' living room. I assume she is angry about the attention Elijah is getting, and when I discipline her, she avoids my eyes and ignores my threats. She hits her legs with her hands and begins to cry. Her whine morphs into a wail. Her hands begin to twitch. She pulls herself up on her tiptoes and screams. The piercing scream leaves her body like a demon freeing itself. She falls on all fours. With no other way to voice her fury, she bangs her head on the floor while I stare in complete amazement.

I am shocked, petrified. "Stop, baby. Stop! You're going to hurt your head!" I fall next to her and try to hold her head back, away from the floor. It only makes things worse as she struggles against me. I try to put my hand under her head to soften her blows. She pounds her head repeatedly around my hands, in my hands, on my hands; anywhere she can make contact. She screams louder.

I pull her close to me in hopes of calming her. She flails against me and pounds her head into my nose. The pain jolts me away from her. I fall to the floor in anguish, reaching for my nose, expecting blood. Amelia continues to bang her head. Her anger terrifies me. My parents have no answers. They are just as lost and confused. None of us can bring her comfort.

Amelia bangs her head for days. I read books, talk to friends, call doctors. Most of them say to ignore her behavior. "She is a normal two-year-old." I disagree. It isn't normal for a calm child to transform into a screaming, thrashing, and convulsing ball of anguish. She is voicing my pain. She is screaming my anger.

She and I are saying the same thing. But she cannot pretend the same way I can. She is brutally honest. I search for answers for days until I happen upon a way to help her: a G.I. Joe doll. She picks him out, a large figure dressed in an Army uniform. His hair is dark, like David's. He's tan and muscular. Amelia's eyes, her entire demeanor, calm. "Daddy," she says.

She clings to "Little Daddy" with small, delicate arms. She curls up with him to read books. She talks to him in her crib. She gives him "smoochers." She carries him to the playground. He swings with her. He rides next to her in the grocery store. They are inseparable. She is still Daddy's girl. Even a glimpse of Little Daddy allows her to lighten her load.

We all watch her, tormented. No child should be taking on this kind of grief. She holds the pain of absence on her shoulders. The painful issues of the war don't pound in her mind, like they do in mine. She has no way to voice the anguish of missing her daddy. She has no way to protest, to write the president, to vote, or even to be heard by one politician. But her two-year-old shoulders still hold the weight of this war.

She sits quietly, eating waffles while I take care of Elijah. She is quieter than usual, and Little Daddy sits right next to her. She says in an overly calm voice, "Where's Daddy?" Without thinking, I say, "He is right next to you, baby."

"Daddy went bye-bye?" she asks, quieter, calmer. She stops me. I think my heart stops beating. Tears fill my eyes. This is the first time that she has dared to presume the answer. She has been preparing herself.

People keep telling me that Amelia is too young to understand, and that she won't even remember him being gone. They say that she will fly through this. They say that it will all be over before she will even know it happened. They are wrong.

She can feel pain. She can feel abandonment. She can feel lost. She can feel alone. She can see the other men in her life here with their families. She can see other fathers holding their sons and daughters on their shoulders at the grocery store. She can see the life that is going on around her while she sits apart. No Army pamphlet could have prepared me for this. I know now that I need to take her home.

"Daddy is playing in the sand. He is bye-bye, but he loves you very much." I don't know what else to tell her. I can't tell her he's at war and that he may be killed at any moment. I can't tell her that her flippant goodbye to him in New York could be the last one that she ever has. I can't tell her anything other than what I know she can handle: He loves her.

She begins to thaw. A smile finally rests on her face. She hugs Little Daddy and says, "Daddy be home in minute." The need on her face replaces my hurt and my fear of being alone. I know now that I can't accept my parents' offer to stay and move in with them. I can't allow them to continue to nurse me through this. She doesn't need my parents. She needs me to be her mother.

We all knew that our stay wouldn't be permanent. I had always planned to return to New York after the holidays, but I had briefly considered canceling my plans and staying with my parents. But now, after seeing her raw anguish, I want to go home. It has been said that "home is where the heart is." "Home is where you hang your hat." "Home is where the Army moves you."

To me, to our family, home is where David's shoes are.

The Long Road Home

Tonight we are leaving for New York, and my father is beside me. We decide to leave at dusk (again) in hopes (again) of Amelia possibly sleeping this time. "You need to try to sleep, Amelia. We are going for a long drive," I explain, trying to persuade her to relax and give in to her tired body. She nods her head and plays with her dolls while she watches the fading scenery from her window. She laughs and smiles. "We go home, Mommy?" she asks.

"Yes. We're going home." She happily returns my smile in the rearview mirror. We've been away for two months. Amelia seems to welcome the opportunity to leave her pain in Kentucky. I wish I felt the same way. Instead, I'm terrified of the reality awaiting me back at the base in New York. My deep fear rises when I'm not paying enough attention: Am I strong enough to be alone with two babies? I'm not sure if I am enough of a mother to compensate for David. I'm not sure if I have the desire to be anything other than miserable without him.

I'm nervous that I won't be able to handle all that is before me. It all feels so burdensome: Taking care of the truck, maintaining the house, nurturing my marriage. All added on top of feeding and bathing the children, taking out the trash, and keeping our house clean. Changing diapers, nursing a baby, paying bills, cleaning up after cats, shoveling snow, salting the sidewalk. Not to mention fighting off every illness and germ hovering and threatening to destroy my ability to take care of my babies. I need to stop thinking about what I am feeling. I need to stop thinking.

Truth be told, I'm scared of being alone with them. What if they both scream at the same time? I've not yet lived alone with both children. My parents have been by my side coaching me and urging me to lean on them. I have been in the warmth of their house for too long. My house beckons, but I am afraid that it will be cold. And I am unsure how to make it a warm, safe place for all of us. But I need to do it, to feel it. I'm not willing to give in. My children need to see that I am not scared or weak. They deserve everything I have.

I don't talk to my father about any of this. He doesn't want me to leave. Both he and my mother want to keep me close to them so that he can fix my truck, she can fix my pain, and they can soften my tears and fears. He's worried, but on the outside he's quiet and stoic. He leads by example. We left my mother alone in her home, but she is thinking and worrying for me. Their love surrounds me like a warm, comforting blanket. I try to focus on the feeling so I can remember it and allow it to carry me through.

I take the first eight-hour shift. "Go ahead and sleep, Dad. I'm fine," I tell him. My heart goes out to him. He promised me two months ago that he would help me drive back to New York. His determination to keep that promise rests in his furrowed brow. He's worked all day, and I know his aching body needs relief. He attempts to stay awake, but after several hours of driving, he finally relents. He sleeps next to me while I listen to music. He sighs next to me as I wish this long drive away.

The road is empty and soft music soothes me. Amelia babbles in her seat, unwilling to sleep. "Aren't you tired, baby?" I ask from the front. She should have gone to sleep hours ago. We have pushed through the night; the promise of an early dawn looms on the horizon. She doesn't answer. She continues to play with her dolls, and I try to step out of her reverie. At least she isn't throwing up, I remind myself.

The snow that was promised begins to fall, slowly at first, but then picking up speed until the road before me is white and unmarked. When the storm was predicted, we knew we would have a slow journey. But my father's plane ticket home, the one that he bought two months ago, only allows for two days getting us there, getting me settled, and then taking him to the airport to tell him goodbye and send him back to work. I would love to stop and wait out the storm, but the guilt I feel for taking up any of his work time urges me to keep going. I stick to the planned, hectic schedule and push through the snow. I slow my pace and pray that the looming blizzard waits until we pass before dumping its bounty. When the truck starts to skid, I pull the wheel slowly, but the truck compensates with a jerk. It fishtails before the tires make contact with snow rather than ice. The truck straightens again, and I find the center of the road.

My father starts from a sleeping trance. He looks out the window in surprise and amazement at all that he has slept through. "Good time for you to take a shift, huh?" I ask him with a chuckle. He steadies himself and takes a drink of coffee to help him fully open his swollen eyes. "I guess this is what I get for deciding to leave on Friday the thirteenth," I say, half laughing. He mumbles a response as he motions for me to pull over so he can take control. I am happy to allow it. Elijah nurses, and Amelia munches on breakfast while my father stretches his legs and urges his body to accept such a small amount of sleep.

He climbs into the driver's seat and puts the truck into four-wheel drive. Amelia chatters about the beautiful snow as we drive through another blizzard. His shift begins somewhat smoothly, but when we slow to five miles per hour on the interstate, I feel a surge of panic set in. The snow pounds the truck, and if we stop, we stand a chance of getting snowed in. We decide to keep moving, and his experience at the wheel steadies my pounding heart. I know he can handle it. But I'm not sure if I can.

I try to stay calm, but my knuckles are white as he pushes through the worst of the blizzard. There is one car in front of us, and there are faint lights of an eighteen-wheeler moving behind us. "This guy doesn't look like he is doing so well," I say of the car in front of us. Before I can say more, his car begins to fishtail, and he slides from one lane to the other before he completely spins. We are now hood to hood on the icy interstate, and I clutch the dashboard as my heart races.

I feel the truck move slightly to the right as my father keeps his cool and makes small adjustments to avoid the same thing happening to us. The car in front of us spins again and is now horizontal directly beside us on the interstate. If we stop, the eighteen-wheeler behind us will crash into us. The car is perpendicular to our truck, and I scream as his tires spin. He is trying, in vain, to get back in the right direction before the truck smashes into him. His hood is inches from Elijah's door, and I am terrified that his squealing tires will find pavement just in time to smash into the door and my sleeping baby.

My father continues to move the truck methodically and carefully. We pull away from the car just as he shoots across the interstate, landing sideways on the shoulder. He is clear of the truck, but his panic nearly cost our lives. I crane my neck to see what happened, but instead see the fear in Amelia's eyes from my scream. "It's okay, baby. Mommy was just playing." She is unsure of my answer, and she stares in silence.

I am speechless. I try to regain some control over myself. There are so many things I want to say, but I find no way to form the words. I stare out my window and try to force the coming tears back into my chest. My father's grip on the situation is tight as he calms my nerves by telling me that he has the wheel and that everything will be fine. I believe him. Because he says so.

I sigh with relief when we begin to leave the sparse traffic behind us and are on our own on the interstate. We inch through the blizzard, the cold, and the ice. All seems well until we see another eighteen-wheeler jackknifed across the interstate from median to shoulder. Other trucks have stopped to form a barrier. We are hours away from Fort Drum. We have been driving for twelve hours already. There are no exits for miles. Amelia hasn't slept, and Elijah will be hungry again soon. "We can't get stuck here," I manage, anxiety deep in my chest. "We've come too far." I begin to chew on my bottom lip. Besides, there's nowhere to go.

"Mommy!" Amelia cries from her seat, and a familiar sense of dread fills me. I look back to her and attempt to calm her, but I am too late. Last night's carrots are already flowing from her mouth. The color drains from her face, and she begins to shake and tremble. "Oh, baby," I say as a desperate tear leaves my eye. Before I can say more, the second wave of nausea hits her, and she explodes. I am overwhelmed. It was inevitable, but I had hoped it wouldn't happen.

My father tells me to turn around and hold on. He pushes our truck over the mounds of snow and into the tiny gap between the guardrail and the wrecked truck. The drivers of the other trucks try to flag him to a stop, but he ignores them and continues to drive over the plowed, frozen snow. When we are clear, I look behind us to see raging drivers shaking their fists in the air. But I don't care. My faith in my father overshadows any guilt that I may have for ignoring their roadblock.

"Mommy, I mess," Amelia calls from her vomit-covered seat. "I know, honey. I will clean you as soon as I can," I tell her. It is freezing, and we can't stop. I can't get her out in the cold. She is screaming and crying. Elijah is now awake, screaming and crying also.

We pull over on the shoulder, and I attempt to clean what chunks I can from her seat. I wipe her face, clean her pants, and scoop the vomit into my hands before throwing it out my open window. I give Elijah one of his teething toys. "Let's just go until we find an exit," I say to my father.

He continues to push through the blizzard until we reach a tollbooth. We are the only vehicle traveling on our side of the interstate now, so the bewildered look on the toll taker's face isn't a surprise.

She questions my father. "Did you all just come through a wreck?" she asks. My father nods slightly, and I can see the concern on his face that perhaps the truck drivers have called ahead to stop us. "How did you get by? Did you have room?" she asks. My father only slightly nods again and hands her the money. I'm sure the smell of vomit and Amelia and Elijah's screams hasten her decision to allow us to pass without further questioning.

We inch through the tollbooth, and I feel myself unclenching and breathing again. "I thought for sure she was going to call the police," I say. My father says little, only that he is glad to have made it through. He keeps his eyes on the road and stays quiet while I try to soothe my children into just a few more minutes of patience.

We continue to drive through the tollbooths, through the snow, and through the ice. He sits next to me making me feel like it will all be okay, like my worst fears are not coming true. But the relentless storm can only be God telling me that I have made the wrong choice.

When we finally reach an exit, my father pulls into a gas station, and I take Amelia into the nearest restaurant. She is cold, angry, scared, and clingy. She cries and shakes. I try to clean her and attempt to calm her. She can feel that I am unsure of myself. "It's okay, honey," I tell her as I take off her dirty clothes. "Does your belly hurt at all?" I ask. "No," she says quietly. I put clean, warm clothes on her, and hold her close as we walk back out into the blizzard. I am anxious to put this stop behind us. I want to put this miserable trip behind us, too. It is tempting to ask my father to stop for the night, but we are in the heart of a blizzard that could continue for days, and I trust his driving experience. Right now, it is the only thing I am sure of. And, I don't want him to pay a hefty fee to change his flight.

Elijah is hungry and crying when we reach the truck. My dad sits quietly next to me in the parking lot while I try to nurse Elijah. He is a hearty eater, and I know that it will only take twenty minutes to fill his belly. I don't want to take him out in the whipping cold when I can satisfy his cries in the time it would take to bundle him and walk him inside. My father gives me privacy by not watching while Amelia climbs all over him. He lets her. It's cramped in the driver's seat, but they giggle and make the best of their tiny play area. She is trying to find something to do while Elijah eats. Or tries to eat.

He screams and pushes against me. Then nudges me as if he is starving. I try to feed him against his protests. He can feel the tension, and it isn't settling well with him. He likes calmness and enjoys nuzzling with me. He likes to watch my eyes while he drinks. My eyes aren't on him. They are on the growing walls of snow threatening to swallow my truck. My dad steps out every few moments to scrape the ice and snow. It is too cold to keep the snow off the truck. Before he finishes cleaning the mirrors and the windows, more snow threatens to freeze and cover them again. He gets back into an overly packed truck that smells of vomit and sour milk.

My father has more patience and understanding than I have a right to expect from him. He is calm, prepared, and unfailing. I am nervous, terrified, edgy, angry, and near tears. He doesn't ask if I want to turn around. He doesn't hint that we should. He sits next to me and calmly waits. I know I am fortunate to have such a father.

After forty-five minutes of nudging, begging, and attempting calmness, I give up trying to nurse Elijah and return him to his car seat. He is content to be back in the comfort of his blanket. Amelia seems happy to return to her dolls as well. We are moving again. It has taken us nearly two hours to go twenty miles.

We keep pushing and pushing until we are close to Fort Drum. We push on because the kids are quiet, content, and finally asleep. We drive endlessly. By the time we reach the exit for Fort Drum, we have been driving for an agonizing eighteen hours.

Finally, on Saturday the fourteenth, the sun breaks through the clouds, and we pull into my driveway in New York. I am riddled with doubt over the possibility that I have made a mistake. Seven-foot snowdrifts, below-freezing weather, very few friends, and no family await us in New York. No David. I have nothing but my wits and my desire to prove I can do this. I wonder what I have done. Amelia all but explodes out of the truck. She runs into our living room, and the light bursting out of her eases my fears and worries. "My house! My living room! All my toys! Mommy! All my toys!" She is smiling, laughing, playing. She cackles.

I feel my father's hand on my shoulder, his backbone inside me, and his heart all around me. I know he's proud of me. As Amelia runs from her bedroom into her living room, I know I've made the best decision for my family. This is the house that David and I have made a home. My father is standing beside me as I begin to really feel like a mother. It is my turn to be the parent and to be the one that stands by them, sits next to them, and helps them through their pain.

He is worn and weary, but he pushes through the little time he has left here with me. My father takes apart Amelia's crib and assembles her toddler bed. He puts Elijah's new crib in my room, checks the tires and brakes on the truck, and helps me go to the store to stock up on diapers, wipes, and food in case I am unable to leave my house for weeks.

When his short and intense stay is over, I drive him to the Syracuse airport for his flight home. I fight the urge to beg him to stay here with me. I want to curl up on his lap and bury my head in the crook of his arm. But I won't.

As he steps from the truck, he looks into the backseat to tell his grandbabies goodbye. He looks me in the eye, and I see him beg me, silently, not to do this. I see his fear and worry. It is all there: his love and his willingness to always take care of me. "Thank you, Dad. I can't thank you enough," I tell him. Tears well in my eyes, and I look away until I can control them. When I turn to look at him again, pride has replaced his worry. Seeing it there causes me to pull back my shoulders and lift my head.

"I know I am doing the right thing," I tell him. I step out of the truck, walk around to his side, and wrap my arms around his broad shoulders. "I love you, Daddy." He kisses my cheek and his scruffy beard scratches my face. He says nothing, but I hear him swallow over the lump in his throat. He gives me one last hug, leans into the truck to wave goodbye to the kids, and turns to walk into the airport. I watch him until he is merely a shadow moving through the crowd. Everything in me wants to call him back to me. But I don't. Because I know he would come.

The long drive home is strangely quiet. Amelia says nothing. Elijah sleeps. I return to my house and my children settle into their home and their familiar smells. All is as it should be.

Anger

"I got a tree on my back

and a haint in my house,

and nothing in between but

the daughter I am holding in my arms."

–Toni Morrison, *Beloved*

Clenched Fists

I am shocked by my anger. I went to endless meetings and mandatory briefings. "How to help your soldier acclimate." "How to help your children deal with an absent mother or father." "How to maintain your car while your husband is gone." "How to manage your checking account while your spouse is deployed." There is no adequate briefing for anger. There is no sufficient Army pamphlet for my rage.

I am alone with two babies because he wanted this job. I am a stay-at-home mother because he wanted this job. I have a non-existent career because he wanted this job. I have a broken belly, a swollen crotch, and I need surgery to repair the damage of two babies pushing their way thoughtlessly through my body. My body. My pain. My stretch marks. My hemorrhoids. My varicose veins. My torn vagina. My blood. My placenta. My broken umbilical cords.

I feel empty and hollow and alone. And insanely angry because he isn't here. Two cries, each of various octaves, let me know that I will never again be alone. They beckon me at all hours of the night. "Mommy!" she screams in the middle of the night, and he cries throughout the night for milk. There is no rest in sight and no release for my fury. He left me for a job. He left us for a job.

My anger controls me like a psychotic puppeteer. I stand in the checkout line at a store and attempt to isolate and hide myself from the world. A woman in front of me is staring. She watches me struggle to keep Amelia content in the cart while Elijah sleeps peacefully on my chest. She knows the look on my face. She sees it here every day with countless other military wives pushing through their days.

But it doesn't stop her from speaking. "Is your husband deployed?" she asks. I want to ignore her. Or yell at her. I want to scream that it is none of her business and I don't want to be reminded of his absence. "Yes," I say with no hint of a smile. It isn't terse enough. She continues to talk. She continues to stare at me with pity, compassion.

"We are so thankful for the job that your husband is doing," she says. "Thank you," I say and walk away. Thank whom? I wonder. What exactly is the job that he is doing? Who is it helping? Who took him?

He took him! He made the decision to join after September eleventh. He decided not to return to the reserves and to go active duty. I went with him and left everything to be by his side. I have given everything to his children to his job to his dream to his love to his affection to his life to his obsessions to his dinners to his breakfasts to his lunches to his clothes to his parents to his sisters to his everything.

I feel betrayed and abandoned. I feel tricked, cheated. I am overwhelmed and short of breath. My mind is consumed by his torment and constantly searches for his laughter. I am always wondering if I am performing. Am I worthy? Am I a good Army wife? A good wife? Does he feel loved? Does he feel missed? Do I fulfill? Do I satisfy?

Why did he leave? Why did he reenlist? Why did he choose this for us? Who is he helping? Do they care? Who is he serving? Who is he making happy? Who does he love? Who does he hate? Who is he working for? Who cares? Who helps him? Who wants to be with him in his hour of need?

Is it worth it? Is all he is doing really worth the pain of our separation or his lonely nights without his family? Is it worth our children having an absent father and me having a vacant husband? Is he who he wants to be? Is this the life that we were meant to live? This isn't the life that I imagined for us. My image is being trampled, burned, and massacred.

I want to run, to escape. I want to abandon and flee all that consumes me daily. But I don't. I stay because I know he has the same questions. He has the same tortured, burning questions bombarding him daily. I love because I know he loves. He loves deeply. He loves strongly. He loves wholly. He loves angrily. He loves tightly. Even when I am too angry to see it, I still feel it.

Two children beg for my affection. I turn to their outstretched arms for solace.

Writing

"**H**ow are you doing with David being gone?" It is the question that everyone feels the need to ask. I have a rehearsed answer: "We're fine. The babies are doing well. I know that Amelia is missing her daddy, but everything is fine. There's only a short time left until he returns." Etcetera. Meaningless conversation.

How do I tell someone that we are broken? We are no longer whole. Because you refuse to serve, my husband is serving for you.

Nothing pulls my anger from the very pit of my stomach more than hearing, "You knew this was going to happen. He signed up knowing that he was going to be deployed." He did know it. I knew it. What we didn't realize was that he was going to fight in two wars in two separate countries. We did not realize that he would be taken from us year after year. How could we have possibly predicted any of it? We did know a deployment was coming. And, because he knew it, he is honoring his commitment. Because he feels pride in his commitment, I say nothing to the person preaching from a stump.

Although we knew he would deploy, there is no way to avoid the pain of separation. There is no way to predict the severity of the roller coaster emotions. Each day brings a new reality. With each realization, sadness follows. People usually tolerate sadness, but asking someone to understand the anger is too much. Since he is part of a volunteer Army, we are not allowed to be sad. We are not allowed to be angry. We are not allowed to question. Not by society. Not by anyone. We are just to push forward, thank the outstretched hand, and say nothing of the fissure in our family.

It isn't as though I don't hear constant words of encouragement or get cards in the mail from friends and family. Wives of soldiers previously deployed tell me to think of the reunion. They offer help and advice. They provide ready shoulders. They are sincere and steadfast. I hear the uplifted prayers for strength from strangers and the local commercials on the radio thanking the military families for their sacrifice. There is enough to sustain me if I could just allow it. I hear it all. I want so badly to fully allow it to engulf me and protect me from myself.

But my anger forms a barrier. It will not allow me to see or hear anything other than my desire for him to be here with us. My children's giggles reflect his laughter. In their lips, I see his smile. In her curls, I see his hair. I see his body. In their eyes, I see his life, his promise to me.

I miss him.

Here, other wives feel the same way. We watch our children. Anger consumes us. Our hearts burn when our children take their frustrations out on us. They ache when we witness our babies' small heaving sobs. Our entire being quakes with anger when our children beg for their daddies to come home. And when they spit words of hate at us when we have no way to promise their fathers' return. Questions of "Why?" and "How long?" torment us. We have nowhere to place the blame. On the soldier who volunteered? On President Bush? On the Iraqi people? On the 9/11 terrorists? On ourselves for loving the soldier?

We have no answers. No release. No sense of an answer coming to us in the near future. We only have the burning questions.

Fallout

David tells me he is fine. He tells me he is safe. He tells me all the attacks on the news are far from him, and that I shouldn't worry. He tells me that the bombings are miles away. The disfigured faces on the television do not belong to his unit. They are from another unit. Sadly, that brings me comfort. And then instant guilt for the relief I feel knowing that David isn't one of them. He tells me he feels safe and that he is distant from any serious danger. I believe him. Stupidly, I believe him.

I tuck the kids in for a nap and sift through the mail in hopes of finding a letter from him. I see his handwriting and drop everything else. I open his letter excitedly. He always writes of fond memories, funny stories, and his hopes and dreams for his kids. His letters are beautiful. I love the thought he puts into each one, and I cherish that he considers handwritten letters timeless and romantic. He could and does e-mail, but this way, each letter is personally written and crafted, read and reread, and lovingly sealed with affection.

This letter holds none of that. He tells me curtly that he was attacked the week before. His truck was assaulted on a routine outing in Baghdad. He says he doesn't want to worry me, but he also wants to be honest and to involve me in his life while he is over there. He tells me of going to the bathroom across camp with his gun. He tells me of hearing bullets fly overhead while walking, that it is common. Rocket propelled grenades have landed in the camp. His letter speaks of random fire throughout the night. He tells me it is all normal and that I shouldn't worry.

Life leaves my body. The papers drop from my hands. I fall to the garage floor and gasp for air. There is no air. The cold concrete floor clutches my hands and refuses to allow me to stand. My stomach churns and sours. I force myself from the garage floor, and I gather his words to me. I read and reread the letter.

The words won't change. I beg them to change. I plead with them not to exist. I implore them not to bring me news that I had prayed never to hear or read. I beg them not to taunt me with the truth and weight of what is happening in Iraq.

Somehow, I had tricked myself into believing he wasn't at war and that nothing could touch him. I hid behind the idea that our love would always keep him from harm and that somehow my love for him could wrap him in some protective, bulletproof cover to keep him safe. Stupidly, I believed if we loved each other more than other couples, God would spare us the possibility of losing him.

I tricked and deceived myself. He helped me. All of the "common" happenings are just now reaching me months after he left. He knew I couldn't handle the brazen and dagger-filled truth. But his promise to keep nothing from me is what finally spilled it from his mouth. I am angry with him for telling me now. I am enraged with him for not telling me when it happened. I am irritated with myself for needing to know. I hate myself for wanting to be there with him rather than here, with my children, pretending everything is fine. Other families choose to know nothing, but I can't live on a "need-to-know basis." I know myself. The last deployment taught me the pain of dropped communication. I have to go through this with him, or I will learn to live without him, this time for real.

As I sit and stare at the letter, I try to go back in time and imagine it. I am sitting next to him during the attack, attempting to feel what he was feeling. I try to imagine his fear or to see his thoughts. I try to hold his hand while he prays that he will be okay. I try. I fail.

There is no way to imagine what it feels like to be shot at. I can never be there with him. I will never be with him when he is the most scared. My heart aches for his pain, and it burns for his fear.

The date on the letter is January sixteenth. It is weeks old. I try to remember that day. What did I say to him when he called? What did we talk about? Was it senseless? What did I say to him the day before he was attacked? What trivial thing did I tell him about the children or about my life? What did I make him feel? Did he go into the briefing of the situation the next day knowing just how much I live and breathe for him? Did I let him know that no matter what happens in our lives, he is the only one who has ever made me happy? Did I tell him that I could never thank him enough for the years that he spent with me? Did I let him know I can never repay him for the gift of our babies?

No conversation comes to mind, and I pray I made him feel loved and missed. I hate myself that I wasn't there for him. I hate that I could not feel it in him. How could I not know what had happened? How could I not hear it in his voice, in his comments, or in his demeanor? He needed me, and I couldn't feel it.

On the floor of my garage, I cry uncontrollably. When the sobs subside, I look around. His skis are tacked to the wall, and his bicycle leans against mine. His snow boots and his winter coats keep watch over me. Our fishing rods stand in the corner, waiting for our next camping trip, and our tent trembles from the cold draft pushing through the crack of the garage door.

Everything shifts. He is at war. I know war means death. Someone will die. But, selfishly, I pray, "Please, God, don't let it be my husband."

My fragile sense of security is gone. For the first time, I consider specifically what may be, without searching for some way to force those painful thoughts from my mind. I may never hear his laugh again or see the wrinkles bursting all over his face when he smiles. I have to live as though I may never again see his beautiful hazel eyes. He may never touch Elijah again or toss Amelia into the air. He may never take them for another bike ride. His promise to teach Amelia to ski may never come to pass. The family camping trip that awaits him may never happen. He may never be here with us ever again, and I have to live every day in that fear. The words "we were attacked today" have changed the stars for me.

My chest tightens, and I wonder if my ability to breathe normally will ever return. We could have lost him. I could have lost my beautiful, sweet, honest, loving husband. He could have died on that road in Baghdad. He still might.

Incarcerated

It is bitterly cold outside. We are completely buried in snow. It is halfway up our windows. I have always loved everything about snow. The way it looks, smells, and tastes. I have always welcomed the serenity of sipping on hot chocolate, and later on hot coffee, while the quiet blanket fell like cotton on pillows. I treasured the feeling of it under my feet.

Now I hate it. The white engulfing me has become my warden. The blizzard outside our window continues to torment us. We have been under attack for days. We are being held hostage by the piercing wind, the icy chill, and the unrelenting flood of thick white from the gray sky. I have to break free from my anger, from my depression. I have to look to my beautiful children for hope. I have to find some joy in my life. Right here, now.

Cabin fever takes the blame. My skin craves the warmth, and Amelia endlessly questions, "When we go outside?" She needs fresh air like I do. We are outdoors types, she and I. We need sun to feel whole and alive. We need to be outside to feel the wind and sun pulling the stagnant air of this long winter from our lungs.

This is my third winter at Fort Drum, my second winter alone. Though, even when David was home, he was out training. Every day is cold, and then colder. Thirty below zero with freezing wind is truly a wicked and devilishly bitter cold. I can't leave the house. The base is on a mandatory shutdown. No one is to be outside more than a few minutes. The soldiers continue to work in their snow gear. My snow gear serves no purpose. It sits on the garage floor, drying from my last attempt to find the sun.

I want David here with me, to watch the snow. To remind mo of my love for it. To snuggle with when the frigid wind finds its way through the cracks of our house. I spend the days playing with Amelia and Elijah. Amelia and I have tea parties with stuffed animals. They all have peculiar and sophisticated names. We take turns putting on powdery pink makeup, and then we make funny faces in the mirror. We chase the cats through the house on our hands and knees, meowing and hissing along the hallways. We make chocolate chip cookies, and we draw shapes in the leftover flour as we wait for them to cook.

Elijah prefers to fly on my legs as I push him into the air, making airplane noises and sputtering sounds. He grins and giggles repeatedly as I cover my face with my hands and then pop out from behind them to say, "Boo!" He finds it hilarious when I dance in front of him to loud music, and he slobbers on my face and hair as I pretend to eat his belly slathered with imaginary peanut butter and jelly.

There is happiness in those moments of imagination, when we are all content and warm, but when their giggles fade and my energy wears thin, I feel the cold seeping into my bones. I need to get out of this house. While Elijah takes his morning nap in the crib and Amelia busies herself by painting on the computer, I go out to the garage and open the heavy, frozen door. Small white waterfalls of snow stream into the garage, but before me is a solid wall of snow. It comes above my waist. The winds dance across my front lawn. They pick up snow, spin traces of it in the air, and then drop it randomly.

With each new gust of wind, the mounds of snow waltz and change shapes. They move from one end of the driveway to the other like white crashing waves moving across an ocean of asphalt. It could be beautiful. To someone else.

I can't take my children out in this. Yet I want to. I want to chance their chapped, raw cheeks. I want to bundle them and take them out to face the pain of the wind and the chill of the wetness. I am temporarily insane with the desire to feel alive. But their needs are more important than mine. I pull the garage door and feel defeat as I watch the daylight disappear underneath.

Walking back inside, I go to Amelia and try to find a smile. She reflects every emotion I have. She watches my every movement for guidance. "Snowing again, Mommy?" she asks from the couch.

I settle onto the couch with her and pull her tightly to me. "Yeah, baby, it's snowing again. Isn't it pretty?"

Fighting for Freedom

This neighborhood is lifeless. The moment the snow stops, I am out the door. No one greets us. We walk out to complete silence. I wonder if anyone is even here. So many women and men leave when their spouses are deployed. Few people want to face the harshness of this cold, desolate place.

With no blizzard to cage us, the kids are in their snowsuits and the truck is warming. I am finally leaving my prison cell. This is my fifteen minutes out in the yard. Of course, I am being watched by the warden, but I have a few moments of freedom to feel life on my face.

"You ready to head out, Amelia?" I ask as she wobbles over to the door. She looks like a pink cotton ball. "Yeah! she squeals. She has been ready for days. Elijah is covered with countless blankets over his car seat cover. I am so bundled up my feet sweat and beg for an escape from my boots.

I open the garage door and face the mountain of snow that has been plowed into our driveway. I should have shoveled it, but I grew weary of shoveling at night, only to find myself plowed in again in the morning. The snowplows have no mercy.

I move to the truck, open Elijah's door, and pin Amelia between the truck and my legs. When his car seat snaps in place, I remove his layers of blankets, close his door, swing Amelia's layered body onto my hip, and walk around to her side. She is already whining. "I hot, Mommy!" she yells in my ear. "I know, baby. Give me just a second," I whisper to her.

Amelia has to come out of her snowsuit as soon as she gets in the truck. She gets carsick when she gets too hot. I have learned this lesson the hard way. There is still a trace of vomit floating in my truck from the last time that I thought I could make it to the store before she got sick. And I can still see images of white, clabbered milk and chunky carrots falling from her mouth. But trying to get her in and out of her snowsuit, while she pushes against me, is like trying to put a fish in pantyhose. We fight until she is finally free, and I am sweating from the effort.

As I finally touch the steering wheel, thirty minutes later, I am ready to go to the commissary, the base's grocery store. I force the truck over the plowed snow and inch out into the icy street. This is the joy of my life right now. Leaving my house just for groceries is like winning the lottery. I have the winning numbers of four-wheel drive and fifty-five minutes before Elijah will breastfeed again.

When we get to the commissary, it is snowing again. I have to get Amelia back into her snowsuit to get out of the truck. Fish. Pantyhose. I am sweating again. The mixture of wetness and cold makes me feel like my face is breaking into pieces. My ears burn. My mind immediately lurches to images of frostbite and black appendages.

Amelia is covered from head to toe. She is a walking pink cotton ball again. Getting out in the snow is a grand adventure to her. She touches the snow with her tiny gloves and giggles as she kicks it with her snow boots. I stop for a moment to watch her. Her innocence brings a smile to my face. I want to play with her, to build a snowman here in the commissary parking lot, but the clock is ticking. I'll have to nurse Elijah soon enough and I prefer to do it at home, where Amelia is free to roam and play as she wishes while Elijah and I cuddle and connect.

I walk her around the truck to get Elijah and pin her, again, between my thighs and the truck. He is sleeping. Not for long. The bitter cold is his alarm clock, and it wakes him. He is crying. His car seat cover has a tiny opening, and the wind whips through the truck, finding his tiny cheeks. I attempt to block the wind, pull him from his car seat, and wrap him in layers of blankets. Amelia is playing peek-a-boo with imaginary strangers between my thighs. She is patient; as patient as a two-year-old can be.

Elijah is not happy, and he squirms under the blankets. He is cold and not asleep. That is a horrible combination for his four-month-old body. He pushes himself into my chest, trying to find a soft spot to resume his disturbed nap. He wails from beneath the soft, blue fabric. Because walking with Amelia and holding Elijah is like walking through molasses with a screaming banshee in my ear, I decide to carry both of them.

I reach down with one hand and scoop her up. I walk through two feet of snow, carrying fifty extra pounds. Every inch of my body is wet with sweat.

I get inside and take Amelia out of her snowsuit. She only pretends to help me. Because there is no other option for me, she has to ride in the cart while I carry Elijah through the store. She is too young to walk, and he is too little to sit.

I thank God for my front carrier. Once Elijah is snugly strapped to my chest, he always settles in for a peaceful nap. However, using it requires unwrapping, re-exposing, and re-disturbing him. Every moment he is awake brings him closer to realizing that he is getting hungry. I attempt to ease him out of his snowsuit and into the carrier without making him more frustrated. This is impossible, but I try anyway. I must try. I need to try. I cannot be a prisoner.

With Elijah finally secured in the carrier, ready to resume his nap, I can now concentrate on Amelia. I have come prepared. She has many snacks to keep her occupied. I pick her up, maneuver her around Elijah's cocooned body, and put her in the cart. She is happy. He is happy. I am tired

I notice that several workers at the commissary are watching me. They are staring with sympathy, but not offering help. But why would they? This is common here. We are all alone. Any offers from them would only be met with my rejection, and they understand my familiar look of independence. That is also common here.

I am down to thirty minutes and counting. I wander the aisles in blissful idleness. We don't need much. I stare from one box of crackers to the next, not really thinking about anything other than the sweet silence surrounding me. All I hear is Amelia's chewing and the faint music playing in the background. No one is crying. No one is hungry. I try to live in the moment.

Twenty-five minutes.

Twenty.

Fifteen.

Elijah begins to stir in his carrier. It's time. I pay and make idle chitchat about the weather. I stare at the children's snowsuits and beg silently for a reprieve. No tears. Amelia goes into hers first. Fish. Pantyhose.

Elijah is reluctant to open his eyes. I try to cover him as much as possible with his snowsuit and blanket without completely removing him from his cocoon. He squirms, and his curled body begins to jerk with movement. He will be wailing for milk soon.

We walk out into the blizzard. It is beyond cold. It takes my breath when the doors open. The icy wind moves into my throat, and my chest begins to hurt. My wet clothes instantly stiffen. I walk in frozen jeans. They are frigid and stiff. I carry both babies again, walking through two feet of snow.

I ask the grocery bagger to wait at the curb while I take the babies to the truck and drive to the door. I can't punish him by making him push a cart full of groceries through the snow. He nods and pulls his toboggan hat over his face. His steamy breath escapes the fabric of his covered mouth.

I put Elijah into his seat while I pin Amelia between the truck and my thighs. Peek-a-boo.

I walk her around to her side and put her in. I pull off her snowsuit while berating her in my mind. Why can't she just ride five minutes home in a snowsuit without puking?

The drive home consists of her endless talk and his screams. He is hungry. She is two. I am alone.

I turn onto my street and merge into my tire tracks, the only ones on the road. Everyone else seems content to be inside. Perhaps they are accepting and complacent. Or not here at all.

As we pull into the garage and I close the door, the long process of returning home and collecting wet, cold clothes plays out. I go to Elijah and nurse him. He is happy to eat and happy to be home in the warmth. When he is full and content and asleep again, I put him in the crib and put a movie on for Amelia. She is transfixed in front of the television. I hate that she has a temporary electronic babysitter. But it is the only way to do necessary chores and to make sure she isn't wandering through the house. Clogged toilets, nostrils filled with cereal, painted walls, and scary "gift giving" to Elijah happen when I try to avoid using the television. The last time I refused to turn it on, I found her hiding in the opened dryer, saying, "He likes it!" over and over again. It took me a few minutes to realize what Elijah "liked" was lint from the laundry room wastebasket.

I go into the garage and collect the groceries. The milk is frozen already. The eggs feel like bricks. I open the door one last time to catch a glimpse of the outside world and stare at the driveway. I will be out here later, shoveling and listening to sleeping kids on the monitor. Someone driving by would actually assume that I was enjoying music on my headphones. Someone would be wrong.

I close the garage door; my cell door. I put away the groceries. The house seems less like a prison after leaving it. Now, I can think about coloring pictures with Amelia and cooking chocolate pancakes for us. The rooms don't seem so small, and I can breathe again.

I sit on the couch, pull Amelia onto my lap, and concentrate on the snow outside. This is what we will be staring at for months to come. It is a pure white that will turn gray, then black. It will eventually become an eight-foot-tall brown, frozen, dirty wall of snow on the side of the road. I don't let myself think about it. It's still beautiful now. I hold Amelia and focus on that.

Overwhelmed

Both kids are sick. They both seem so big and independent, until they vomit. Then they become delicate flowers that need nurturing and constant affection.

I might be sick too. I'm not quite sure. I don't have the luxury of being sick. What a pleasure it would be to have a person caring for me who would tell me to relax and take a warm bath. The thought of someone actually handing me a cup of soup to eat alone at a kitchen table, rather than spooning some funky shapes out of Amelia's soup bowl, is nearly intoxicating. Kid's chicken soup; I wonder exactly what it's doing for my soul. This is our gourmet meal of the week.

All of last night was spent running between their rooms. She was crying and coughing and asking for me. He was crying and vomiting and needing a new diaper. He had a fever. She was feeling left out because she didn't have a fever. He needed medicine every four hours. She wanted medicine because it tastes "yummy for my tummy."

In one day, nearly thirty dirty diapers and Pull-Ups hit the trash. I exist on twenty minutes of sleep. I want a continuous supply of caffeine, a direct line into my veins. Coffee loaded with caffeine calls to me with tantalizing aromas. But it has been three years since my last taste of it, and I fear what it would ignite in my body. Not to mention Elijah's. Instead, I need an IV of determination with a prescription for patience.

In a word, I'm miserable. And it's all David's fault. Why would he choose this lifestyle for us? Why does he think he needs to be doing this? Why is he always leaving me? Why doesn't he have to deal with sick kids with overflowing diapers, explosive coughs, dripping noses, and projectile vomiting? Why is it that he is never here when we need him? I know I am not the only wife to question. But his putting his life on the line to put food on the table brings terrifying images and unimaginable pain.

Who is he serving? What is it all for? Why can't he just be a normal dad and husband and stay close to us? Why can't he just be here every night? Why did he join the Army? Better yet, why did he reenlist? Why would he sign those papers in Iraq, knowing my hands were overflowing here? He already knew what it meant. He did it again anyway.

I want to keep plugging without feeling any resentment, anger, sadness, tiredness, or complete exhaustion. I want to see a light at the end of the tunnel, to focus on what I know to be true. I chose this life with him. He didn't tie my hands behind my back. He did not push me to believe in his agenda. I walked into it with him. And I walked into this reenlistment with him. But because I am the one always left behind to pick up the pieces, I can't think rationally. I can't concentrate on my role in this decision. I can only focus on the frustration and anger that engulf me.

Two sets of weepy eyes, with more need for me than I can possibly meet, look to me for comfort and direction. But that is hard to muster when at the end of my tunnel is another deployment or a trip to the field. Staring me straight in the eyes is another training school or something completely un-family-oriented. When he is home from a deployment, he isn't home. He is working. He is always working. He is gone for months, training for his next deployment. There is no time for me to be anything other than strong. But my steps are awkward and dizzy right now. I have no strength left in my aching limbs.

I try not to say anything about this to David when I talk to him. We're both scared by the very real idea that he's missing a life with his children and wife. We both want that life, the one where he comes home every night and wakes us every morning. It is the one where we all sit together for breakfast and laugh about cream cheese on Amelia's nose and cereal all over Elijah's face.

But we have to focus on the life we have now. I clean vomit and diarrhea, and attempt to comfort two sick children. I try to hold two babies who need me; two sweet babies who constantly need me, and I try to cuddle them with their fevers, diapers, medicine, thermometers, vaporizers, and humidifiers.

I have only ten minutes with him on the phone. Ten short minutes to describe how the kids are feeling. Ten minutes to listen to his problems, his worries, his fears, his hate, anger, and sadness. Ten minutes to help them all three feel like a family, to feel like father and children. And also to feel like a wife, and to make him feel like a husband. He has ten minutes to let his children hear his voice. Ten miserable, wonderful, achingly short minutes.

I cannot tell him how angry I am with him. There is no reason to put a burden on him that is unfair to carry. We do not discuss how lonely I am without him or how exhausted I am. I cannot tell him how overwhelmed I am by the babies; by the sick babies. I am saturated by the ever-crying, never-quiet, all-consuming babies. I cannot tell him any of this. How can I? We only have ten minutes to feel like a family.

Necessary Evil

Elijah and I share an addictive habit. We love to cuddle together at night and sleep on David's side of the bed. I love to hear him sigh. He takes in deep breaths and smiles happily as he exhales. He likes to be close to me. He snuggles his little head into my shoulder, and stuffs his tiny fists into the warmth of my chest. I hold him on his side and curl my legs around his tiny body. I'm intoxicated by this. Like a baby junkie searching for my hit of snuggling. It's the only time when everything feels exactly right. His nuzzling body and his sweet moans let me know I am doing exactly what he needs and wants. There is no guesswork or uncertainty, and it is the only time of day when the anger and frustration that I have leave my body.

I look forward to the end of the day, just to lie next to him and feel his sweet breath on my face. I feed them both, bathe them, and then sing and read to Amelia before she falls into a deep sleep. She only allowed me to hold her for a few months when she was a baby, and she has always been an independent sleeper. I relish what Elijah is giving me with devilish delight. I am thankful to have it.

And I am beginning to regret it. Both children go to bed at seven o'clock. She sleeps better that way, and he is exhausted by then. He only wakes once a night to nurse, so I am happy with their schedule. The problem is he will not stay asleep for most of the night without me at his side, so I am locked into going to bed early. I cannot move without waking Elijah.

I hold him in the nook of my arm while he sleeps peacefully. When I move, even the slightest bit, he cries. I can't get up to use the bathroom or roll over when I get uncomfortable. I can't readjust him or watch television. I can't read with the light on, and when Amelia has a nightmare, I can't get up to go to her. I can't do anything but lie on my side and hold him. When I do give in and move, he screams. Then she screams. Then I want to scream because it is three in the morning and the house is awake.

Though I love the comfort of my baby next to me, I need time to myself at night. Time to decompress, to read, to listen to music, to write, to watch mindless television, to talk to friends uninterrupted, or to eat in peace without feeding him and helping her.

It's time to have Elijah sleep in his crib at night. The crib is in my room, and I will wake him if I sneak into bed—alone, always alone—after he's fallen asleep. So I decide to sleep on the couch until David comes home. It seems a much better fit for one body.

The first night, I'm prepared. I feed them and bathe them. I read and sing to Amelia, and then I rock Elijah before attempting to put him in the crib. I sway softly while singing to him, and then I ease him down onto the crib mattress. He is happy. He is cooing and playing. Until I walk away.

His screams are quiet at first. They are tolerable. "Mommy! Why is Jah crying?" She is at the end of her bed. "Give him his nuggie," she says. I reply, "He has his pacifier. He is getting used to his bed just like you had to get used to yours." I hope I convince her. I haven't convinced myself.

"Oh," she says. I walk back into her room and tuck her in again. I kiss her nose and watch her settle in for the night. I stare into her deep brown eyes, and I see her screaming, two years ago. I hear her wailing, and my mind floods with guilt that I let her cry.

I try to push it to the back of my mind and chalk it up to being a first-time mother, but as Elijah's cries burn in my ears, I hear her newborn screams all over again. Guilt and frustration fill me, and I can't help but believe I let her down. Behind my closed eyes, it all unfolds, again.

She bit my nipples. She gave me mastitis. She gave me a fever. She gave me nothing. She took everything. My belly, my husband, my perky breasts. She took my life. She took. She took. She took.

She cried constantly. I blankly stared at her during those weeks and wondered how I could ever be both mother and father when I hated being mother. Days became nights and nights became hell. I wondered if there was ever a time when she was content.

Amelia continued to cry while her bloated belly twisted and turned with painful gas. I read books on how to settle her stomach. I paced the floor with her and put her belly on my forearm while I prayed for just minutes of sleep. I put her in her crib and let her cry. I stared out the window while she wailed, and I wondered how I could be a normal mother or if I was sane after having visions of throwing her through the glass and into the snow.

I had a master's degree in education, but could not understand or reason my way through this. No amount of school could have prepared me for her deafening screams. I tried anything and everything until exhaustion turned into exasperation. When walking didn't help, nursing didn't work, and ignoring created more tears, I finally fell onto the couch. I reached for her flailing, pink body, and found that she calmed almost immediately when I put her tiny body in the crook of my arm.

Days became weeks. She liked to sleep on the couch with me. I let her. She let me. We developed an understanding about the crying. She didn't cry anymore, and I didn't throw pacifiers at her anymore. She breathed softly on my cheek while I finally found sanity and peace in blissful sleep.

Those few months that we were alone were the only times she let me hold her. And now, as I look at her sweet face, I hate myself for not giving in to her need sooner and feel guilty for not instantly being the mother that she needed and demanded. She educated me.

I want to linger in her room, to hold her while she sleeps to make up for all those times I didn't. But she won't allow it. "Go, Mommy," she tells me.

I close her door and hover in the hall next to my old room. Elijah is wailing. He is trying to pull himself to stand, and I want to run to him and crawl in bed with him. He rarely cries, and this sound in his voice is new. He sounds abandoned.

Instead, I walk into the living room and hug myself, trying to convince my rambling mind that I am not failing him. I am not reliving my mistakes with her. This is necessary. This is for the best. This will keep me from losing my mind and both kids will sleep better. And maybe I will sleep better.

I tell myself anything to appease the guilt in my gut. I walk to the clock. It has been five minutes. It feels like he has been crying for hours. I stare at the ceiling and feel the anger return. Why isn't David here to help me? This is a job for both of us. If he were here, I could talk to him about it. If he were here, I wouldn't have to torture my child. We could take turns sleeping with him.

I sit on the couch and turn on the television, flipping through the channels mindlessly. Nothing can hold my attention.

I pace the floor and walk to the clock again. Seven minutes. A lifetime. I call my mother and ask her to tell me again why I should do this. She tells me gently and firmly that I have to do something to find time for myself. She reassures me that he is fine and that he will be fine. I hang up with her still feeling sick to my stomach.

Back to the clock. Ten minutes. I begin to wonder how ten minutes feel to him. Maybe he thinks I've left. Maybe he thinks I'll never go back in there. Maybe he thinks that just beyond the door is an abyss that swallows his parents whole when they leave. I need to go back in there.

I walk to the back of the house and stop myself. "Don't go back in. It will only make it worse." I have read it everywhere and heard it everywhere. I will only make it worse. How could it be any worse?

I open Amelia's door instead. She's fast asleep. Little Daddy is next to her. I close her door softly and return to the living room. I glare at the clock. Twelve minutes.

I have abandoned my baby. I have broken his heart, and he will never heal. He wails, and I cry.

Enough. I run to his room consumed with desire to hold him. I stop myself in time to avoid a collision with the door. There's only silence. I wait for a moment, and then crack the door enough to see him sleeping in his crib. He is curled up with his stuffed animal and is sighing happily. I walk in and stand over him.

I am relieved. And heartbroken. This is the first time he has gone to sleep at night without me. This is the first time I have walked out on him. This is the first time I have broken his heart. I reach down and touch his soft cheek. Part of me wants him to wake just to see him reach for me. The realistic part of me is grateful. He is happy and content. And he is not in my empty arms. I close the door softly behind me and leave what used to be my room.

I walk into the kitchen, search the pantry, halfheartedly, and try to find something for dinner. I settle for soup. I sit at the table, alone, and stare into my bowl.

I have lost my appetite.

Bargaining

"She could lose everything:

herself, or worse,

her children."

—Barbara Kingsolver, *The Poisonwood Bible*

Repositioning

F our months have already felt like an eternity, and I will do
anything to make time go by faster. Especially when it involves
what has been here all along. It is time to cherish what I have before
me: my kids. I need to cheer for them, laugh with them, and push
myself not to think of David. If I learn to appreciate what I have
and make the best of it, maybe God will reward us with a shortened
deployment. I force myself to leave the anger behind and focus on
plugging into their lives and enjoying my time alone with them.

Amelia is happy with my resolution. She and Elijah are now the
center of my world, and my tunnel vision is allowing them to shine
fully. Amelia started gymnastics today. We are taking a mommy-
and-me class together. With Elijah strapped to my chest, I stretch,
shake my wiggles loose, and walk the obstacle course with her. She
is blooming right in front of my eyes, and I love witnessing it. I welcome the bittersweet excitement of seeing her change, and I try to
overcome the need to still see her as my tiny, delicate baby.

When David left, she was still a fragile little baby. Four months have brought so many changes. Now she is tall, slender, and moving like a child. She runs and flips and jumps. With bated breath, I watch as she walks on the balance beam. She is unsure of her step, unaware of her ability. She reaches for the teacher. She holds her hands tightly while she takes tiny baby steps across the beam. She leaps from the balance beam, jumps, flails, falls, and crumbles, laughing.

She runs around the obstacle course, sure of her steps, until she reaches the balance beam again. She steps onto it, holds out her airplane wings, and then reaches for the teacher. Again she is unsure.

I try to step away and allow her some distance from my overly protective grasp, but I want to run to her and coach her through every step. I want to keep her close to me and never push her away. I want her never to step away. I want to keep her in my pocket, my ever-growing pocket. But to do so would deprive her of this delight. She is so proud of herself. She looks over her shoulder to make sure I am watching. And I am. More than I ever imagined I could.

She attempts the balance beam for the third time, and I suck in my breath, nervous for her. She holds the teacher's hands, but just at the last moment, she lets go. It is only for a few seconds, and I am the only one to notice.

She immediately looks to me for approval. Elijah and I squat to hug her. She pushes my eager arms away, and I can only stand back to clap for her and cheer her on. My baby is tumbling, flipping, jumping, playing, flailing, and falling. All by herself.

I am thankful I am here to see it and thrilled to witness every moment of her metamorphosis. To see her changing and to witness her becoming sure of her ability is truly a gift. For too long, I haven't been paying attention. I have been focused on what we have lost. Now, I see her fully and clearly, and she brings me pure joy.

It's still there, though. It won't go away, but I won't let it engulf me: The same small voice that constantly says, "I wish David were here to see this."

Getting Caught

Comparing David's day-to-day existence with my own is not helpful. Yet I cannot help myself. His situation is clearly more dangerous. In the moments when I'm not completely distracted by the needs of my children, I realize I should always be more concerned about him. Thinking about how he is, about his safety. That is the way of the Army wife. My fear and feelings come second to those of the soldier.

But when I see from the instant messages that he's leaving the computer to go nap, or to go eat, or to have a cup of coffee, or to work out at the gym, I am crazy with jealousy.

I nurse Elijah while I type, feed Amelia her breakfast while David types to me, and potty train her in between. I clean and cook. I change diapers, clean spit-up, shovel snow, cut grass, and run errands while he talks to me of being bored, listening to the same music, having a growing mound of books to read, and having too much time alone. He naps. When he has downtime after his missions, he goes to the gym twice a day. He stops at the chow hall to see the lunch lineup. He visits the newly built PX on camp for his shopping needs. This jealousy feels wicked and toxic. It feels disgusting.

I drink decaffeinated coffee while Elijah clings to my breast. I listen to children's music while cooking, cleaning, typing, doing laundry, and searching for Elijah's elusive pacifier. While folding clothes, I daydream about new crayons, invent ways to ease teething pain, cleaning diarrhea, and how to coax spit-up off my new black shirt. Long gone are my discussions about politics, Harper Lee, and rich Southern fiction.

Obviously, he isn't on vacation. He isn't lounging in a hammock, sipping champagne, and reading a magazine. He wants so desperately to be a part of our everyday lives. We want it, too. And I try to accommodate him.

"I just don't see how you are doing it," he says. "No problem. I'm used to it," I respond. There's nothing else to say. I can't tell a soldier in harm's way that I am jealous of his situation. I can't tell him I want to take a nap or that I'm tired when he has been up for hours patrolling the streets of Baghdad.

His naps aren't pleasant. Surely they're filled with bombs, thoughts of missions, me, our kids, and our families. If I feel guilty, his guilt is that much more, since he made the decision that brought us here.

He is weary and scared. And it all eats at him day by day. Each time he comes to us on the computer at the morale center on camp, he stares at the children longer, tells us he loves us more, and he begs the monitor enforcing the thirty-minute maximum for just five more minutes to watch us. She paces behind him, tapping him on the shoulder to remind him that other soldiers are waiting for the computer.

It's agony. Yet, a piece of me would trade with him, just for a moment, to gain his perspective. I want the opportunity to miss my kids, to ache for them. Because he knows that ache, because he has that perspective, I am jealous. I know he would give anything to be in my situation; to be next to his children just to smell them again.

He wants to hold Elijah against his cheek just after a bath, to change the dirty diapers, or to run to Amelia when she cries. I know he wants to watch Elijah struggle to roll over onto his stomach and that he wants to see their growth. I want it for him, too.

Because I know he aches for these things, I try to push my frustration down deep inside of me. I try to hide it from him and bargain with God: If I push these things into the pit of my stomach, David will have to come home. If I swear never to utter these feelings to him, he will be safe and unharmed.

He knows. "I'm sorry. I shouldn't have put you in this situation." The concern on his face is obvious. His tired eyes look into the computer screen. His apology leaves me feeling ashamed and full of guilt. I don't want to feel this way. And I certainly don't want him to take the blame. It isn't his fault. He did originally sign the papers knowing that he would be going to war, but remembering his stories of being a young child pushing tanks around the floor and building forts for his little green Army men makes me responsible too. I love the image of that sweet child. It is that image that I see in him still. Being in the Army is his childhood dream, and I want him to have it. I can't shatter it with weapons of hate, bitterness, and jealousy. I know he is searching for a way to make his job and his family fit together without pain.

"No need to be sorry. I'm fine," I say. Embarrassed. When it is finally over, hopefully these wandering, broken, scattered puzzle pieces can somehow find their way back to each other to be whole again. We all need to feel purposeful again. We all need to be a family again.

Pay Off

My days are spent searching for the joy in the little things. I cling to Elijah's smile. My ear is finely tuned to Amelia's laughter. I dance with elation when Amelia learns a new skill, and gasp with amazement as Elijah grows and changes on a daily basis. Those tiny moments are worthy of rejoicing because they are what keep me from thinking of our overwhelming situation.

We push through the days of breakfast, lunch, and dinner. And Amelia and I discuss what we will do for the day. This morning, as I prepare breakfast, Amelia is nowhere to be found. Her hungry belly usually propels her to the table, and her continuous circles through my legs as I cook remind me she is eagerly awaiting her food. This morning, I move through the kitchen without stumbling over her. Sweet singing echoes from somewhere in the back of the house.

I'm curious, but relieved to hear singing. When she's totally quiet, she's usually up to no good. I stop cooking to search for her, and as I wash the flour from my hands, I hear the sound of little feet running on the hard tile.

"I poop, Mommy!" she says with wide eyes and an enormous grin. These are the words I have been waiting to hear for the past five months. I have begged her to poop on the potty. I have bribed her, pleaded with her, chided her, pulled her, pushed her, and finally, given up on her. In true Amelia style, she had to do it herself.

She curls her tiny fingers around my index finger, and pulls me toward the bathroom. "Come see poops, Mommy!" she says. I walk with her into the bathroom, expecting some kind of miracle poop to be awaiting me or to hear angels singing as rays of light beam from the small potty. "Show Mommy your big girl poops!" I shout.

She takes my hand and pulls me to the potty. "Look, Mommy. Poop!" Tears stream down my face. She has won the Stanley Cup for pooping. The announcer roars over the crowd as I stand to cheer her on. "Ladies and gentlemen, may I please have your attention. We have a special surprise tonight, folks. Little Amelia has just pooped in the potty," he says as the hushed crowd listens intently. "Come on. Let's give her a hand, folks!" I hear as I hover over the tiny green and white potty. There, staring up at me, are two jelly-bean-size pebbles of blessed poop.

"You pooped!" I scream, jumping up and down. She could ask for a million dollars and I would mortgage my entire life to give it to her. "You get two stickers and two jelly beans." And a car, sixteen popsicles, forty-three fruit bars, you name it. If I had the world on a string, it would be hers. "I can't wait to tell Daddy," I say to her.

She hears "Daddy," and the wheels in her head start turning. She runs out of the bathroom muttering something about Daddy and cameras. Her little feet pound the floor again as she runs back to the bathroom.

In her hand, she has our web cam. It is unplugged and turned off, but it is her only connection to David. It is his preferred method of voyeurism. It is his only way into our lives. She holds it over the potty and says, "See, Daddy? See Amelia's poops?"

My daughter, the genius. My daughter, the miracle pooper.

"Let's take a picture to send Daddy," I say to her. She stands with pride next to her potty. And then begins to fidget and whine. "What is it, baby?" I question her. She looks at me with surprise.

"I poop again," she says. She pulls her stool over to the big toilet, heaves herself up onto it, and proceeds to work potty magic. She is quiet and serious. Then, she looks at me with those twinkling, beautiful brown eyes.

"You pooped again!" I scream. "I poop again!" she shouts. She picks up the web cam and holds it over the toilet. "See, Daddy? See my poops?" she asks the gray camera.

I take countless pictures of her standing next to the potty. Sitting on the potty. Holding a sign that says, "I poop, Daddy!" Pointing at the pebbles in the potty. Within minutes those poop pictures are on their way to Iraq. They are images of life going on. It is a small victory in our family, and I know they are going to the only other person in the world who will well up with tears when he sees them.

Chest Pains

David calls nearly every day. He tries to call in the afternoon when the line isn't as long. Soldiers usually wait in line to call just after they eat dinner. He is eight hours ahead of us and between two and four in the afternoon in Baghdad he knows that our early morning has started already. Hearing his voice always makes the day more bearable.

But there are times when we go to the store or leave for just a moment, and I miss his call. I dread seeing a flashing light on the phone if I have been out running errands. It usually means that his voice will be on the other end, sounding down and broken, telling me he is sorry he missed us. Sometimes he tries for hours just to get through one time. With other soldiers waiting for the same phone, he can't call again to try my cell phone.

We have walked in and out of the house for two days now, and no blinking light has greeted us. I am worried and terrified and pacing. I try to maintain my composure. I do laundry, nurse Elijah, and Amelia and I have long conversations about her dolls needing new diapers. Nothing pushes the time. I attempt to gain some perspective and try to convince myself that he is busy. He will call.

I have to find a way to keep the pressure at bay. When I begin to unravel, my children can feel it. They can feel the insanity floating through the house and settling in the cracks. The fear that he has been hurt overwhelms me.

When the phone finally rings on day three, I run for it in a panic. "Hello?" My voice squeaks and betrays my attempt to be composed. "Hi. This is your husband's roommate," a strange voice on the other end stammers. I am confused and worried. My heart stops. "David wanted me to call you to let you know that he is sick. He is on quarters so he won't be able to call you until he is allowed out of the room." I feel the color return to my face, thankful for his kindness.

"Is he okay? I mean, is he just vomiting or something?" I ask. "He is having chest pains. Not sure what's going on with him. He will call you when he can." He has nothing more to say. He is terse; he doesn't know me well enough to chat. I want to bombard him with questions. I want to know if David is having a heart attack or if he is panicked. I want to know anything more than he can tell me.

"Thank you for calling. I really appreciate it." I hang up the phone and attempt to occupy my mind. I wander aimlessly for two more days. We have become accustomed to talking to David. Amelia wants to tell him that she likes to color with markers, and that Elijah is wearing new shoes. I want to hear about his day and to tell him about mine. I need the release of telling him.

When the instant messenger doorbell rings on the third day, I run to the computer to see his smiling face. He looks sallow and thin. "Hey there!" he calls from the screen.

"Are you okay?" I cover my ears with the headphones and listen to him breathe. "Yeah," he answers, "I think I just had food poisoning or something. I ate some local food, and I'm not so sure that was a good idea." His grin will not allow me to chastise him. I want to tell him to take care of himself and then yell at him for worrying us. I want to be next to him to hold his hand and baby him with homemade soup and prescription cuddling.

"The kids have about gone crazy with me. Amelia is so cranky," I tell him. "Put her on here," he says. I cover her ears with the headphones, and she begins to answer his questions. I recognize the smile on his face and know that they are telling Daddy-Amelia secrets. His mouth moves methodically, and her intense gaze is fixed on the computer screen. There are soldiers behind David, laughing and staring. I pull one side of the headphones away from her and try to eavesdrop on their conversation.

I hear the words and instantly recognize the song "The Sound of Silence" as David sings into her ears. She sways with his voice, and my heartbeat slows with each verse. She listens to the entire song, and finishes the serenade with, "Again, Daddy!" He laughs, and complies as his mouth begins to form the words again.

When she is finished, she hands me the headphones. She is smiling. "What made you sing that?" I ask. "Don't you remember? That was the only song that calmed her when she was a baby," he responds. He smiles as he recalls the endless nights of soothing her with Simon and Garfunkel. He used to spend hours alone with her in the living room while I attempted to sleep. She would scream until he put the melodic song on repeat. I smile. My chest isn't so tight anymore.

"The next time she gets out of control, just play the song," he says. His smile widens. "Thanks," I say. I hold his gaze for several minutes. "It's good to have you back," I whisper into the microphone. He grins and winks. He spends the remainder of his time watching Amelia drift back and forth in front of the web cam and laughing as Elijah plays in his swing.

Losing the Battle

I am strong, alone, independent, and terrified. My anxieties are rising again. The weather remains brutal and unforgiving. With frigid ice holding us in place, even leaving the house causes instant fear and worry. I walk out into the snow to get our mail. Walls of shoveled, frozen snow surround me, and there is ice everywhere. "Please, God. Make every step perfect."

It takes nearly ten minutes to get to my mailbox. Stepping lightly, stepping slowly, and stepping softly. I slip. Then regain my balance and contemplate the next move, looking carefully for each break in the ice. There, three feet from me, is just one inch of concrete so that I can corner and manipulate my foot.

I have my monitor with me. Always. It is attached to me. From the speaker, the babies softly breathe their contented moans. They are soundly sleeping. I am in the snow and ice trying to get the four days of collected mail. I have been a prisoner of the weather for too long. There are letters from my husband out there.

By the time I reach the mailbox, I know that I will not make it back. It has taken an eternity to get to this point. I look at my open garage door and wonder if there is any way I can retrace my steps to get back to the safety of my couch. Nothing can happen to me on the couch. Nothing can take me from the babies on the couch.

I attempt to repeat my moves, putting the tip of my boot on what looks like a piece of black concrete. When I start to slip, panic takes hold of me. There is the instinct to protect myself. I attempt to twist my body over so that I can catch myself with my hands, but the ice is too much for me. I fall hard. I fall quickly.

My head cracks against the pavement before I actually know what has happened. I wonder for a moment if my head has broken open. Just after the crack, there is a dull thud, then a burning sensation. I feel wetness at my neck and wonder if I'm bleeding.

I can't move. I won't move. My body won't let me. A sharp pain shoots from my head to my back. From my back to my feet, a burning sensation is on a racetrack moving from the nape of my neck to my foot, then returning to my neck.

I lie there for what seems like years. The monitor is next to my hand, and the babies are still sighing and breathing. Outside there is silence. Everything that is alive and thriving is inside.

The dark sky stretches out before me. The storm is over. There are only brilliant stars above. There is no moon. Only wispy traces of clouds move through the air. It is eerily quiet. There is only the sound of lullabies playing on the CD players echoing through the night.

With no movement of life around me, the thoughts hit one on top of the next. I could have a concussion. I could need stitches. I could be paralyzed from the neck down.

I stuff my hands into my pants. I usually keep my phone in my pocket. Where the hard plastic should be, there is only a pacifier. If the phone were with me now, I could call my family. I have the kind of family that would move heaven and earth for me. But, they are fourteen hours away, and the phone is inside on the kitchen counter.

The realization of all that this deployment entails for us begins to push on my chest, and I start to wheeze. I am panicked. I am uncontrollably panicked. I am doing this alone and my babies are too young to even dial a phone. They can't help me. My friends who are miles away can't help me. The neighbors who have left town can't help me.

Motionless and broken beneath the still sky, I imagine the babies waking in their beds in the morning. They are cheerful. They are rested. They are hungry. They are thirsty. They have dirty diapers. They are in their beds calling for me. I don't answer.

Thoughts of my sweet babies being alone and scared push me to move. I twist and turn until I am on my hands and knees. My head burns. It is throbbing, bleeding, swollen, and aching. My hands move through my matted, bloody hair until I find the source of pain. It is meaty.

With no strength to stand, I crawl back to the open garage door. I pull the door closed behind me and inch into the light of my kitchen. The sudden light disorients me, and I hold my head to contain the spikes of blinding pain. Once again, I feel for the back of my head. When I make contact, needles push against my skin and shoot through my head and into my back.

I pull myself through the house, step into the shower, turn on the hot water, and watch as it runs red, pink, and finally clear. The throbbing is relentless, but I will need no hospital. I need no stitches.

I search the house for painkillers and make a potent cocktail of ibuprofen, ice, and sleep.

A New Shade of Gray

In the morning, a ray of sun spills through the window. My head throbs, and I pull myself from the couch onto the cold, hard floor. I walk to the window, calculating my steps. Every beat of my heart pulses in the back of my head. I feel for fresh blood and only find crusty, brown flakes of last night's battle.

I move toward the ray of incoming sunshine. My house only gets one ray of sun throughout the day. It is a cave. No matter how many windows I open, or how I crane my neck in order to feel a new day dawning, I have to bask in the glow of a three-inch ray of warmth.

I walk to the light and pull back the curtains. The sky is blue, and the reflection from the snow blinds me. Thousands of colors sparkle in the fresh blanket of white. They captivate me, and a smile forms on my lips as I think back on my childhood love of everything winter. I remember the feeling of the snow beneath me as I pushed it aside making snow angels. I can still smell the hot chocolate in my mother's kitchen as I pulled off my wet winter clothes.

A soft movement to the left of my house catches my eye, and I twist and turn to catch a glimpse of someone or something battling the depth of the snow. Two large eyes stare at me, and I suck in my breath. Her fur is thick, coarse, and it looks like velvet shining in the light. She is the first doe to come this close to my house.

Her eyes are black and they stare back into mine without fear or regret. She doesn't mind that I am watching her. She doesn't mind being disturbed during her morning walk. She is proud, statuesque.

It feels like hours pass as we stare into each other's eyes. She doesn't walk away. She doesn't blink. She stands nearly three feet from me, and her steely gaze captivates me.

"Mommy! I get up now." Amelia's cry from her room breaks the silence, and I run to get her, forgetting about the lingering pain in my head. "Amelia, there is a deer outside! Want to go see it?" I ask. She jumps up in her bed and pulls herself to her tiptoes. "I want to see deer," she says.

We run back into the living room, and I lift her to the window to show her my find. We both press our heads to the cold glass in hopes of seeing her. "Oh no! I guess she went away. We will have to try to see her again some other time." Amelia wiggles free from me and runs to her room to get toys. She is no longer interested in my deer. But I am enthralled by her. I look for several minutes hoping to see her again. She is gone.

Elijah is awake, and he cries from his crib. He has gotten chunky, a gorgeous, healthy chunky. His winter coat is soft, creamy, and pale in the morning light. I lift him from the crib and bury my face in his chubby belly. He curls his body around my head in glee. He smells the way I once imagined snow to smell.

I put him in his saucer, and I watch my children play together while I make them breakfast in the kitchen. Amelia feeds Elijah imaginary cereal, and he opens his mouth like a small bird waiting for a worm from his mother. She giggles after every spoonful. He cackles.

"Hey, Amelia. Want to go out and play in the snow today? It'll be fun!" Her eyes widen, and I have my answer. I look out the window in hopes of seeing the doe once more. There is nothing there. I am alone again.

Extra Care Packages

We love sending David packages. We search for new things to buy. I spend time thinking of what I would want in his situation. He was excited about the neck massager. He enjoyed the nose trimmer. He loves the constant supply of hand sanitizer and moisturizing cream. We relish his excitement and gratefulness when he talks about our gifts to him.

I don't love trudging through three feet of snow juggling an awkward box, one child strapped to the front of me while holding the tiny fingers of another. I don't enjoy the long walk through the post office parking lot with whipping winds and vengeful sleet. I can't stand the hour wait in line with two crying children, listening to countless other crying children.

But excitement in David's voice makes the long mailing process worthwhile. He always has new requests, and I always try to accommodate them.

"Have you gone shopping for the next package?" His voice is delayed more than usual on the phone this morning. Someone talks on the line in another language. I answer, "No. Not yet. What do you want?" I wait for his response. Nearly two minutes later, I hear, "I need some tampons." I sit quietly for a moment to hear his explanation. There isn't one.

I'm not sure if the delay is jumbling his words, but I wait a second longer to avoid the frustration of talking over him. There is silence. "Did I just hear you say tampons? Is that what you said?" I wait for nearly twenty seconds until I hear him. "Yep. Tampons." I try not to laugh. I have an arsenal of jokes ready to fire at will. My tongue itches to snap comments over the twisted wires of the foreign phone. My shoulders twitch, and the laugh is deep within my belly.

When he is silent again, I seize the opportunity. "Do you need plastic applicators or cardboard?" I convulse with laugher. Tears leave my eyes, and I hear his delayed reaction. He giggles and attempts to calm my explosion. We only have a few more minutes on the phone, and he can't waste time.

"We use them to plug bullet holes." It takes a few seconds to reach my brain. My heart falls into my stomach, and I stumble over my apologies. "I'm sorry. I didn't realize." There are no words for how much I can't stand myself.

"No! Don't apologize. I never thought I would say those words either." He tries to help me recover. He laughs to ease the situation, but I am immediately somber and disappointed in myself.

"Do you need any special kind?" This time my sincerity can't be mistaken. "Does the absorbency matter?" I feel awkward asking these questions as my mind fills with images of bleeding soldiers. "Nah. Just try not to send a lot of pink," he signs off, trying to stay light.

I hang up the phone and finish breakfast. I get the kids ready and leave for the store. We buy David the usual: candy, chips, hand sanitizer, and lotion. I add a portable fan and move to the "personal" aisle, trying not to think of him inserting a tampon into a bleeding hole in his body. I want to cling to his last words of humor.

When we return home, we carefully and artfully stuff his package with goodies, letters, and tampons. Dreading the long wait in the post office, I bundle the kids, then free Amelia from her snowsuit for her two-mile drive, re-bundle her when we stop, strap a swaddled Elijah to my chest, and trudge through the snow to the post office. It's freezing. The wind stings my face, and Amelia ambles beside me, stopping to stare at icicles.

We reach the door of the post office and fall into line with the rest of the bundled children and waiting spouses. Everyone mills about and glares at the clerk at the counter. She takes her time with each package and talks excessively to every person in line. People rarely casually venture out around base in this weather, but you can always count on a long line of waiting spouses determined to send a piece of home to their soldiers in Iraq and Afghanistan. They come out of the woodwork to show their love and devotion. Rain, hail, or snow, they are there, waiting. Trying to feel connected, married, and like a functioning family. The post office becomes the third wheel in a marriage suffering from a deployment. Today is no exception. There are countless spouses with packages, and my kids and I stand in line behind the waiting people ahead of us. And many people file in behind us, allowing the cold air to hit us with fresh force each time the door opens.

"We sent Daddy cotton balls in flower box," Amelia tells the lady behind us. An expression of complete confusion engulfs her face, and in some attempt to help Amelia, I explain that David asked for tampons.

A look of realization washes over her face, and her shoulders begin to convulse with giggles. I laugh with her and say, "That's one conversation I wasn't expecting." She continues to giggle with me, and through heaving breaths explains that her husband asked her for baby wipes to clean his gun. We both burst into teary laughter.

"My husband asked for pantyhose," a woman down the line interjects. We both stop giggling and look to her for an explanation. "He says that he needs them to keep the sand off his computer, but I'm not so sure," she says with a smirk. "You know they get lonely," I say. We all three laugh, real and heartily, again. Our loud interruption produces stares and head shaking from the clerks behind the desk. We bring it down to a quiet chuckle. I meet the ladies' eyes around me, and relish the smiles on their faces.

When we finish mailing David's package, I gather the children and prepare to meet the cold outside. I cover Elijah's head with his hat, and maneuver him to the side so that I can bend down to help Amelia. She never wants help with her gloves, but she always cries with frustration when she can't manage to get her "short finger" in the correct spot. On my knees, with Elijah dangling from my chest, I wait patiently as Amelia tries to "do it myself." When she is finally ready to scream in frustration, she allows my eager hands to help her.

I feel eyes watching me in the line. They aren't staring. There is no glaring. They are merely watching and allowing me to do this myself. We all understand that need to do it ourselves. It is what binds us together. The line is long and filled with awkward packages and crying children, but each woman meets my eyes with knowing understanding. I stand, readjust Elijah, and wrap my hand around Amelia's tiny, gloved fingers. I meet their eyes and welcome their supportive nods as we walk back out into the world.

Out of My Hands

People constantly try to offer me words of encouragement. "It will be over soon." "It is in God's hands now." "He will be fine." "Concentrate on things you will do together when he gets home."

I hear it from friends and family. Even from strangers at the mall. They want to help. But nothing helps. None of them can bring him home. I smile, thank them, and walk away. It isn't their fault. They can't understand that although I know God's hands are capable and full, mine feel empty. These hands were tied to David's during our wedding. They held his scruffy face while I kissed him. My unsteady hands cut the thick curly locks from his head when he entered the Army. These hands gently took his baby from him as he walked away from us and walked toward a war.

I want his hands here, back in mine.

I will push it to happen any way I can. When David calls, I ask constant questions about his return. "I heard a rumor today that you may be home in May! Is that true?" He sighs and my heart falls. "Don't buy into those rumors, honey. There are so many floating around here that it just gets annoying after a while." The frustration in his voice almost stops me from asking more questions.

"Do you think you'll have to be there for the full twelve months?" I know the answer. I know what he will tell me, but the constant desire to ask burns in me. I need some idea of when this will be over. We need some sense of hope to carry us through.

"All right." He relents. "Here is what I have been hearing. Don't take it to the bank because I just don't know how true it is." He is quiet for a moment, and I hold my breath in hopes of hearing that they will be home early. "The word down the line is that we are getting extended for the full eighteen months. I don't know. Maybe not. That is just what I hear." He tries to soften the blow of his words, but they are like bricks. I am silent.

"Look, it doesn't matter one way or another. None of us will know when we are coming home until we are about three weeks out. Even then, it still may change. Just expect the worst and hope for the best." I roll my eyes at his suggestion. I can't expect the worst. Thinking of the worst will only hinder my ability to function.

"David, I just don't work that way. I need a light at the end of the tunnel even if you have to make one up!" I feel the tears coming and force them back.

"I know you do. I want one too. It's not so great over here, you know! My bed is empty without you. Amelia's dolly is collecting sand. I can't keep the sand off anything! And Elijah's clothes don't smell like him anymore," He says. "I feel like I can't get the sand out of my lungs! It is getting old over here, too." He is angry and yelling. It startles me. There is silence between us as I wait for more from him. He is quiet.

"I'm sorry. I know you are tired, too," I tell him. He sighs and pushes the frustration out of his voice and replaces it with kind, gentle words. "It doesn't matter when I come home. Just know that I will be there as soon as I can." His words pull at my heart. "I love you, babe. That's all that matters." I feel a smile on my face as he begins to sing the words he has sung for years. "All you need is love. Love is all you need." My load lightens.

"Don't you get tired of that song?" I ask.

"Nah. It just has a way of sticking in my head." I know he is smiling, and we laugh and joke through the rest of the conversation.

I hang up the phone with a sense of hope. Now, when Amelia asks when her daddy will be coming home, I have a response. "Daddy will be here as soon as he can, honey."

No words can bring him home. No amount of offered support can substitute for his charming grin. Nothing about being without him is okay. But he's right: We haven't lost each other. And that might not be all I need to keep fighting through this, but it is enough.

Searching for Normal

We have come into our own. The kids are on a routine. I am on a routine. We make each day merge into the next. We push through it and promise not to focus on who's missing. We are meshing, and I am becoming more confident in my abilities.

Each day, I cook three meals. I clean the babies. I love them, hold them, kiss them. I discipline them, play with them, and laugh with them.

They are intriguing. I find myself rotating around them in awe, watching their every move; witnessing their growth enthralls me. The rate at which they learn is astounding. I am feeling good, feeling clear. I am thankful to feel anything again. I am no longer numb. I accept the winter sun for what it is, and I know the promise of spring is coming.

On days that seem less frigid, Amelia and I play in the snow while Elijah's sleeping sounds echo from the monitor. We push through the walls of snow and crumble with laughter as she tries to lift her foot high enough to step through it. "Mommy! Help!" she cries, and then giggles with me. I catch her just before she falls into the snow. With it up to my knees, I'm afraid she would be completely covered if I didn't. I wrap her in my arms and pretend to accidentally fall into the mounds of snow. We stare into the sky, and I feel her tiny heart pounding with excitement.

"Want to build a snowman, Amelia?" Her answer is always the same. "Frosty!" she says with a toothy grin. We work to roll and form the snow, and we put baby carrots on his face. She loves her white playground, and I love watching her pink cheeks curl when she smiles. My babies are the center of my world now, and I am happy to revolve around them.

They aren't just my children anymore. They are my friends. I have searched their minds for months for ways to heal the pain of an absent father. But it was my pain that got in the way. And, now that I have begun to heal, I see them better. Just before Elijah throws a tantrum, I can deter him. Before Amelia can ask for something, I can hand it to her. I am moving again. I am grooving again.

Hours have become days and days have become weeks. The clock is still ticking, but I am not ruled by time anymore. David is gone. There is nothing I can do about it. The slow realization of this fact has nearly made me insane, but now, I am smiling involuntarily again instead of forcing it every time.

I don't wait by the phone all day in hopes of hearing David's voice. He has developed his own routine, and he tries to call every morning during breakfast. I don't have to worry about missing his calls or coming home to messages from him on the machine. If he doesn't call during breakfast, he is on a mission and will call in the afternoon. Routine is the saving grace of our lives.

He seems safe. His voice makes him feel close. His words are comforting. It is almost as if he is just down the street, and we are waiting for him to walk through the door.

We bombard him with a constant flow of packages. We spend hours drawing pictures for him. Amelia loves to paint for him. We make footprints. They delight in the tickle of the brush on their feet. Their laughs are infectious. "Do again, Mommy," has become my favorite saying. Her gorgeous curls bounce up and down as she laughs and twists from the brush's stroke. Elijah's anticipation overwhelms him. His whole body convulses and his eyes widen when I tell him, "Here it comes again," just before I tickle his feet. His giggle is pure innocence.

Amelia writes David letters. She spends hours coloring them. She fills me in on the details of some, but most of them are "secrets" passed only between the two of them. She paints him dripping pictures drenched with watercolor paint, and she works tediously stringing beads to make a necklace for him. She sends him gifts of used Band-Aids and beef jerky.

I write letters. Every week I write a new one. I write long, involved, descriptive commentary about our days, our weeks, and how much we love him. I give blow-by-blow details about their changing hands, their growing feet, and their questioning eyes. I write of their triumphs, their boo-boos, and their evolving language.

I write of lonely nights and of endless mornings without him. I talk about new improvements in the house and of the ever-growing mounds of snow. I tell him about fixing leaky faucets, cleaning the garage, painting used furniture for the kids, and checking the fluids in the truck. I tell him about the long winter nights that turn into long winter days and of the beautiful sunsets just outside our door. I write of the deer that graze next to our window and the green trees that protect the back of our house. I tell him about Elijah's growing temper and of Amelia's growing patience.

I send Elijah's clothes and socks so David can see how much he has grown. They smell of lotion, of diaper rash cream, and of strained peas. I know David will hold them close to him and sleep with them. He will smell them and smell home.

We make videos. Amelia dances in front of the camera and sings songs. She repeats one line over and over again and then curtsies after her solo performance. She always follows her performance with "Tada!" and a bow. I stand over Elijah and video him while he plays on his activity mat and catch his tiny smiles on film.

"Smile for Daddy, little man." He grins and laughs. "Amelia, can you show Daddy how to do a handstand? She just learned this the other day, Daddy." I talk to David like he is in the other room.

She puts her little hands on the floor and kicks her feet only inches from the ground. She stands up and puts her hands in the air. Her eyes are wide with pride and excitement. "See, Daddy?" She looks straight into the camera and blows him a kiss.

We feel like a family again, functioning. We talk to David on the computer. We can see his beautiful face, and he can see Amelia dancing. She twirls for him. Elijah, in his saucer, attempts to bounce. David can see the jerky movement on the web cam. He can see Elijah's questioning look as he begins to realize that it is his feet causing him to move up and down. David laughs. His smile is real. He is part of us.

He is with us listening to me feed Elijah and watching me tickle him. He is listening to Amelia's new words and infectious giggles. He is with us as they lie on the floor while I mark their growth on a chart. He is with us gasping when I hold Elijah's feet up to the screen to show how they have changed. He is with us as Amelia stands in front of the computer and shows him how she can dress herself. He is in our house again, telling her that she is a princess and that Elijah is his little man.

Date Night

I have a date tonight. I first got word of my rendezvous a few nights ago. The voice on the other end of the line was deep, unfamiliar, and abrupt. "Your husband has requested a teleconference with you on Tuesday at four in the afternoon," he said with little emotion. "Can you be there?" he asked.

"Of course," I responded.

"Be at headquarters fifteen minutes early, then," he said just before he hung up the phone.

I turned to Amelia. "We got a date with Daddy, baby!"

I've bought new clothes. I've bought the kids new clothes. Amelia's hair is in ribbons, and Elijah is wearing a new white sweater. Normally we can see David for thirty minutes of monitored time on the computer, and he can call us through the Fort Drum operator for ten free minutes of conversation, but this teleconference will be uninterrupted, with no dropped reception and no monitor hovering over David's shoulder. We will have him all to ourselves. And we only get one teleconference per deployment. Two if we are lucky.

We walk into the building at three-thirty, and sign in with the soldier at the front desk. It's the building where he works when he's not deployed, and Amelia has been here before. She automatically walks toward his office. "No, baby. Daddy isn't in there," I tell her. She's confused.

I guide her to the small teleconference room, armed with snacks, an infant carrier, toys, drinks, burp cloths, and extra clothes. We only have forty-five minutes with him, but that is an eternity in toddler time. I am hoping that what I have brought her will keep her motivated to stay in the chair and talk to him.

I hardly got situated in the room before I hear his voice calling out to the children. "Hey Amelia and Eli! Daddy has been waiting here for you for an hour! I was so excited to see you I couldn't wait!" His voice oozes happiness as he and Amelia begin to have conversations about her pink dolly, Little Daddy, and snacks. She sits in a chair next to me and munches on crackers while I situate Elijah. I hold Elijah up to the camera, and show David his new shoes, sweater, and pants. "He looks like a little man sitting there," David says. "Look at his little sweater!"

Elijah coos, and Amelia eats and plays contentedly for a few minutes. I offer her toys. She plows through them. They are boring for her, and she resorts to crawling under the chair, searching through the desk drawers in the adjacent office, and attempting to open the door into the hall. I try to force her back into the chair. She isn't interested. "No. Don't want to! I want go home." She pushes out her bottom lip, and sets her jaw in determination.

I look to the screen to apologize to David. A falsetto voice flows from the speakers, and Amelia freezes. David's head has disappeared from the screen, and Amelia's pink dolly has taken his place. It is the same pink dolly that David took from Amelia's room. Amelia looks from the pink dolly in her hand to the one dancing on the screen. David's head pops back onto the screen, and he smiles.

"Mommy, Daddy has dolly too!" She is mesmerized. She spends the rest of her time listening as Daddy's dolly talks to hers. David's dolly talks about the sand in Iraq and about how much Daddy snores when he sleeps. She mentions the letters that Amelia sends to David and the clothes that smell like Elijah.

Amelia talks to Daddy's dolly until our time is finished. David spends time telling Elijah goodbye and thanking me for coming. "I wouldn't have missed it. You put on a good show," I assure him. He smiles, waves goodbye, and we watch as he and dolly leave the room.

"Daddy's dolly at work, too?" Amelia asks.

"Yeah, dolly is in the sand with Daddy, but they always have time for you." I feel myself breathing peacefully, her hand in mine as we walk. She babbles about David and dolly and the Daddy television. I listen and nod as we walk back to the truck. The sun hits my face, and I welcome the warmth of the day.

Reading Between the Lines

The kids are asleep, the cats are fed, the trash is out, and I run frantically through the house trying to get myself ready. Tonight is my weekly book club meeting. Sometimes it is canceled for work, or for illness, but I still prepare myself every Thursday night for conversation about our latest book. I try to remember the exact passages that I want to discuss, and I try to force my mind from diapers and rice cereal long enough to focus on adult conversation.

I sit at the computer for what feels like hours. I have my notes, and I am ready to delve into the characters and plot. Twenty minutes pass, and I begin to wonder if we aren't meeting again this week. Then, I hear the buzz of the instant messenger. It is three o'clock in the morning in Baghdad, and he tries to pretend he isn't tired.

"Are the kids asleep?" he asks when we both settle in with our microphones and web cams. "Yeah," I say, excited. He settles into his chair, pulls out his black-framed glasses, and opens the worn copy of *The Poisonwood Bible*. "Do you remember where we left off last week?" he asks. I search my memory. "I'm not exactly sure. We were discussing the daughters, I think."

"I'm starting to understand why you sent this book with me," he says. Before he left, he asked if I would pick out one book that helped define me as a person. "Think about it for a while. I want the one book that just knocked your socks off," he said. The very idea that he would want to know excited me. But, trying to pick just one proved impossible.

I walked over to our bookshelves and allowed my hands to run over the new and worn spines. My hands grazed the names of Shakespeare, Bobbie Ann Mason, Toni Morrison, William Faulkner, Louisa May Alcott, James Joyce, and Margaret Mitchell. Characters like Harry Potter, Hamlet, Scout, and Miss Jane Pittman begged to be released from the shelf.

"There is no way I can choose just one," I told him. He laughed. "I knew you wouldn't be able to do it. How about you get five?" he asked. "Pick five books that helped define the woman you are. I want a chance to see a different side of you while I am in Iraq," he explained. My mind immediately raced with possibilities, and I spent weeks trying to pick out the perfect books for the assignment.

Now, as we begin to immerse ourselves in the Belgian Congo with Barbara Kingsolver, I feel that same twinge of excitement. "Are you enjoying this book?" I ask him.

"Well, I have to say that Ms. Kingsolver has put me a little too in touch with my feminine side," he says, laughing. "I'm so wrapped up in these women. I catch myself getting so emotional when I read it."

I laugh. "You asked for it! Just remember that."

We settle in to discuss characterization, plot, and theme. He pretends to be interested in my relentless analysis of each character and dissection of the subplot. I pretend not to notice the boredom on his face while I rattle on. "You lost me about three sentences ago," he says when I take a breath.

"Sorry, I think I am talking about something that happens in the end. I'm kind of rusty. It has been a long time since I read it," I tell him. "And you have my only copy."

He laughs. "It is my own little cheat sheet," he says.

"What do you get out of it?" I ask, trying to take the attention from myself.

"Well, the writing is great. I feel so involved. I feel like I am watching it all happen," he says. "But, what I am getting out of this more than anything is the pain in the family."

"How so?" I ask.

"It's the father," he says. "I hate him. Sometimes I just want to rip his head off."

"Really?" I ask. "You're getting into this book more than I ever imagined."

"It's because he is so wrapped up in himself and his job," he explains. "He keeps putting his wants before his family, and they are all suffering. Sometimes I get so angry I wind up just throwing the book," he says.

I wait a moment before I respond. "You aren't like that, David," I tell him. "You won't ever be like that." I try to take his focus from what I know is eating at him.

He listens, and nods. "I know," he says.

"Do you want to quit reading it?" I ask.

"What? Are you kidding? I can't stop now! I have to know what happens to these women," he says with a smile.

We spend the rest of his thirty minutes on the computer talking about the writing, the story, and predicting an ending. I know there are other books he would rather read. My tastes rarely reflect his. But, I love him for doing it. For thirty minutes on a random Thursday night, I am not a mother or a wife. And he is not a soldier in Baghdad. He is, once again, my friend. He is my best friend, sitting thousands of miles away from me talking about books and imaginary characters, taking me far away from my reality. I push through each week, trying to get to our Thursday book club meeting. Even if the club only consists of two old friends.

Answered Prayer

I stare into the mirror for what seems like the hundredth time today. My reflection has changed since he left, but the new wrinkles and lines still mirror my excitement. A sparkle has filled my eye again. I have on new makeup and new perfume. I have a new haircut and new jeans. I have a new body, a new attitude, a new perspective, and new hope. He is coming home today for his two weeks of leave. It has been six months since I last touched him. Kissed him. Hugged him.

Other wives tell me the two weeks aren't worth it, that the pain of telling him goodbye again will be too great. They say the confusion will destroy the kids, especially Amelia. I pretend to hear them. I nod my head in agreement as they tell me to decline the leave. But I can't. I need to see him. I need to touch his hair again. Their words fall on deaf ears.

But I am nervous about him coming. What will he think of me? Will he be as excited as I am? Is his stomach jumping, lurching, cringing, and churning?

I rehearse every moment of our reunion in my head over and over again. How will I respond to him? What will I say? Will I be beautiful to him? Will he notice my new body, my new hair, my new makeup, my new perfume, and my new clothes? Or will he only see the tiredness, the new worry lines, and the wrinkles?

I go into Amelia's room and wake her. "Get up, baby. We are going to pick up Daddy! Daddy is coming on an airplane to see you!" My excitement engulfs her. She jumps to the floor and runs into the living room. "Come on, Mommy!" she calls. "Wait, baby," I say going after her. "You have to get dressed."

We spend an hour getting ready. Elijah is wearing a new sweater vest. The blue in it picks up the vivid color of his eyes. They are sparkling pools on a summery day. He has on new shoes. He kicks at them, and becomes entranced by the new laces. He looks so handsome. Amelia is wearing a sundress. She calls it a tutu. She calls every dress a tutu. She feels beautiful. She spins and twirls and watches herself in the mirror as her dress lifts and falls and curls around her. I spin with her. I feel beautiful. We are his two beautiful girls.

We arrive at the tiny airport an hour early. The lady behind the desk disapproves of me. For some reason, my excitement makes her angry. "Is the flight on time?" I ask. There is only one flight coming in today.

"Yeah," she mumbles.

"Do you know where it is right now?" I want to know where he is in the world.

"I said it was on time. That means it is on time." She sneers.

I stare. And breathe. She can't know we have been through so much pain without him. She can't see my anguish that continues to hide just beneath the surface. She doesn't know what we have endured without him. Still, I want to scream at her, to shower her with all the anger I have needed to dispel. But, nothing will bother me today. He is coming home for two weeks.

"Sorry. I'm just so excited," I say with a slight smile, trying to kill her with kindness. It doesn't work.

"You know, you really aren't supposed to be inside the airport. You are lucky that I am letting you." Her eyes are beady and cold.

My lips tighten. My heart pounds as I consider jumping over the counter and smacking her. "Thank you. It is too windy outside for the kids. Seems like spring is never coming." I try to be pleasant, to push the corners of my mouth into a smile. She answers with a grunt. Nothing will bother me today.

The hour that looms before me is like torture. I try to keep Amelia excited and interested in the day. I fail. The sign that we made for David falls to the floor while she climbs on the chairs. She jumps from chair to chair and chases a fly that taunts and eludes her. I let her jump. I let her play. It makes the lady more agitated, but I would let her do anything to make this hour go away. The lady stares at me from behind her perch. I smile and nod and say, "Nice jumping, Amelia! Catch that fly!" She stares. I glare. Nothing will bother me today.

Elijah is tired of his stroller. He wants out. He wants to jump like his sister. He wants to chase the fly. He wants to do anything but sit. He wants to scoot around on his belly, but I don't want him to get his new clothes dirty. I take him out of the stroller and pull his plump body onto my hip. He rests his head on my shoulder and sighs.

Forty minutes have crept by, and Amelia's hair is falling. And her daddy's sign is getting lost in our jumbled mess. "His plane is coming in if you would like to go outside and watch," says the lady behind the desk. She wants us out of her waiting area. I collect our scattered things, pick up both children, and run outside.

His plane is coming and I can hardly stand. I want it all to be perfect. I want to be perfect. I want his reintroduction to his children to be perfect.

The small jet roars onto the runway. The wind whips and tangles my styled hair, and Amelia's bow is nowhere to be found. I am reeling with excitement, and Amelia is playing in the grass. She plays and throws her shoes in the air. Her dress has grass stains on it, and her feet are bare in the cold grass. She has lost her shoes. The plane is only feet from us behind a metal fence. She is flailing and skipping about trying to find her shoes.

"Daddy is here, honey. Put on your shoes." I try to get her to come over to see the plane. She becomes obsessed with the shoes.

I finally see the blue of her sandals buried in the grass, and I bend over to try to put them on. She kicks my hands away. "Let me do it," she says. Frustrated and unwilling to battle with her, I pick her up and run back into the terminal, clutching the shoes, juggling Elijah on my other hip, pinching David's sign between my fingers, and leaving the stroller outside for the wind. I nearly drop her while trying to unload my arms. I am crazed with the desire to get everything just so.

Amelia cries, "My shoes! My shoes!" I hate her shoes. I try to put them on her. We just have a few more minutes until we see him. She is like Jell-O on the floor, rolling around and hiding her feet from my probing hands. "Mia, please, put on the shoes!" Our things are strewn across the small waiting area, and Elijah is pushing against me, begging to be set free to roam as he chooses. Somewhere, within all the mess, is the sign we are supposed to be holding as he exits the plane.

"Hello." I hear him from behind me. My heart stops. His voice is like music. My hands aimlessly and mindlessly contort and push her shoes. They are disconnected from my floating mind. I don't see him, but I hear his melodic voice. I hear his perfect, loving, velvety smooth voice. I hear his scratchy, I-am-nervous, I-don't-know-what-else-to-say voice.

I fall in love all over again.

My heart pounds in my chest. I can actually hear the blood come out of my heart and swish swish swish through my arteries. The sound of the plane buzzes in the background. People stop, stare, and whisper about us. I hear my breath going in and out of my body.

My mind floods with memories of my life with him. I am holding his hand while his grandmother is dying. I am listening to him mourn her. I am holding my diploma next to his on our graduation day. I am standing before him dressed in white and he is holding my hand. I am drinking him in. He is promising to love me. I am standing next to him while he enlists in the Army. I am watching his pride push through his chest. I am holding his hand. He is telling me to breathe, to push, and to hold on through the pain. He is wiping the sweat off my forehead. He is holding her. He is walking with her through the house singing to her. I run to him crying and shouting that we are going to have another. He is lifting me off the ground in his joy. He is holding my hand again and breathing with me again. He is pushing with me again. He is holding his son, his beautiful son. He is laughing.

He is home.

I am lost in him. I have no words for him. He looks beautiful. He looks tan. He looks worn and relieved. He looks bigger, stronger, and weaker. He kisses me and I taste his tears. Maybe they are mine. Maybe they are his. They are ours. We own them. I can't get enough of him.

He breathes in, taking one long, deep breath. He is pulling my scent into his nose. It is a habit and it is one I have come to love. I return the favor. We are two animals getting reacquainted. He smells sweaty, tired, excited, worn, salty, dirty, and beautiful.

He pulls Elijah from my hip, and he finally holds his son again. A son that he doesn't know. He takes the time to look at Elijah and study his features. Then immediately pulls off Elijah's shoes to touch his feet. "His toes are so much stronger," he says. He touches Elijah's hair and skin. "He is so soft. I haven't felt anything soft in so long." His eyes drink Elijah in. He is intoxicated by him. He closes his eyes and begins to sway. He nearly falls, and I watch his boots move to steady him.

He stares lovingly into Elijah's face. Then, his face moves from sweet joy to anguish. "Melissa, I had no idea his eyes were blue. I should have known that. I am his father!" He stops himself. His chin quivers, and I move next to him in some attempt to stop the avalanche that is just behind his eyes. I have no idea how to stop it. I am useless.

"I just—" He stops again. His eyes water as he pushes his words through his clenched jaw. "I just never expected that kind of detail to be stripped from me." He grinds his teeth, trying to control himself. He clears his throat and looks away. I put my arm around his waist and hide my tears in his shoulder. He shakes, and I search for some way to stop it.

His pain shocks me. I am instantly angry with myself. I wanted him to be prepared. I spent hours writing about tiny details. I videoed every little moment I thought he would want to see. I never thought to fill him in on the obvious details. I took it for granted that he knew. I should have known better.

I desperately want to stop it. I search for the right words. "You okay?" I stammer. Then berate myself for saying the wrong thing.

"Yeah," he says quietly. He pulls Elijah in closer and clears his throat again. He kisses Elijah's small forehead. Elijah's eyes sparkle, and he giggles with delight. "I'm here, now. Right, little man?" The anger and resentment slowly melt from his face, and I sigh with relief.

Amelia stands next to me, holding my leg and watching my reactions. She is puzzled by my tears. I reach for her. "Mommy is so happy, honey! These are happy tears," I tell her scared face.

David turns to her. He wants her to be happy to see him, to run into his arms. He wants to force her not to be angry with him. "Hey, Amelia! Daddy just got off of a big plane. Did you see it?" he asks her, hoping to ease her back into his life.

The uncertainty leaves her face, and I sigh with relief as she runs to him. "Daddy." It is all that she can say. It is all he needs.

He is shocked by her. "Look how long her hair is! I can't believe that. It is so curly! The last time I saw her, she had straight hair!" He strokes her hair with his strong hands. He holds her chin in his palm while she beams at him. His children have grown without him. A web cam could never capture what he has missed.

Finally, he swings his eyes in my direction. I hold my breath and wait for what I know will be the most wonderful reunion of my life. He has left us before. He has left me before. But, this is the first time that he has nearly been taken from us. These hugs and kisses feel different. They feel saturated. They feel heavy. They feel grateful. And they feel deeply thankful.

When our eyes meet, I feel faint. I have stared into his eyes countless times before. I have studied every detail of them. I know every strand of the yellow starburst in his hazel eyes, every red line.

These eyes now stare at me with a new hunger, a new awareness of what it is like to be tired, weary, lost, angry, hurt, joyful, and scared. It all flashes through his eyes. It is all of the emotion that he can never put into words, all within those beautiful, exotic eyes.

He says nothing. He doesn't have to. I don't need any words from him. He has said it all. "You ready to go home?" I ask him. He smiles and nods.

I feel every painful moment of the past six months spill out of me. My mind relaxes. My heart begins to race. My hands tremble as his fingers intertwine with mine. They are familiar. They are callused. They are rough and strong. They are beautiful.

My two children, so small, are back in his strong arms. They are laughing full belly laughs that I haven't heard in months. I can feel the small twinge of fear that wants to creep into my mind; that wants to tell them, "He only has two weeks. Don't get attached." But I push it deep into my mind and make it disappear. I know it is there, but for the moment, it doesn't exist.

We settle into the truck. I look over at him, not really sure if I am dreaming, and Amelia says, "Daddy home?" They are the words that I have been aching to say for what seems like forever: "Yeah, baby. Daddy's home."

Disconnected

It's strange having David here with us again. He keeps telling me I have moved things. I suppose I have. He walks through the house like a dazed stranger asking where things are. "Do you still keep the pots down here?" "Are my razors still in the bathroom?" "Where are the keys to the house?" "Where is the chair that used to be here?" "Could you change his diaper? I can't quite get it right." He fumbles Elijah's diaper as if he has never changed one. He used to do it without looking. He has forgotten, though. Diapers and Pull-Ups are no longer part of his vocabulary.

His vocabulary has dwindled. He doesn't have much to say. He cries a lot. But his tears have no emotion behind them. It is as if they are forcing themselves out in some vain attempt to help him. But nothing helps. He stares. He listens, but he is not involved. I can tell that he is pulling away from us. He is trying not to get attached again. I don't think his heart can stand it if he does.

He stumbles through the day. He doesn't know what either of them eat, or what size clothes they wear. He doesn't know if Amelia needs help on the slide. He tries to put her in a booster chair for dinner. She revolts.

"No, hon. She doesn't sit there anymore. She has her own chair at the end of the table." I put her in it, and she glares at him for his mistake. He shifts his gaze to the floor. He can't comprehend that things have changed without him. He can't understand that we had to go on with our lives. I've been here all along, and even I can't understand it. It seems as though Elijah should still be a newborn in his daddy's arms. The last time David held Elijah, he was a newborn. He is now eight months old.

He examines the tiny changes of Amelia's walk, and the new wrinkles on Elijah's legs. He revels in Elijah's ability to pull himself across the floor. He desperately wants his son to learn to crawl while he's home. Elijah fights and screams when David tries to help him to his hands and knees. David says he doesn't understand Elijah's stubbornness.

David spends hours making a potty chart for Amelia. He wants to see her new ability and wants to reward her with stickers and jelly beans. I don't tell him she has been more than ready for her "big girl panties" for months. I didn't let her wear them until David came home. I wanted him to be part of the excitement. It takes effort to coordinate all this, and that in turn keeps me continuously working from behind the curtains.

I catch him sitting at the table, staring at his children, and trying to hold back his angry tears. There isn't a dam big enough. He cannot contain them. He is scared to touch the kids. He is too terrified not to touch them. He doesn't know where he belongs. He is a stranger in his own house, afraid to be alone with his children. Amelia's words are hard to understand. He's not sure what to do when Elijah cries. If one or both of them gets hurt or sick, he won't know where the medicine is, or how much to give. He is scared that if he begins to acknowledge all that he has missed, he'll never truly be with us again.

Elijah tolerates David and laughs when he is tickled, but it's as if he's a friendly neighbor. David watches him in his bouncer and laughs when Elijah smiles. David hands Elijah to me whenever he begins crying. He can't do the same with Amelia, and she is not making it easy for him. She's angry with him. She doesn't want to sit with him, and she won't hug him. She stands between my legs and watches him from afar. It breaks my heart.

She is unsure of him. She has seen him for months on a computer. For him to actually be able to touch her is foreign. It is foreign for both of them. I give him things to do with Amelia. They plant flowers together. They make necklaces together. They go buy a fish together. She once only had eyes for him, and I will do anything to turn those eyes back to him. I thought that I would once again be jealous of his return. I thought that I would resent him just as I did when he came home from Afghanistan. But their hurt has replaced my selfishness. I long for their broken bond to be mended. I race around, trying to make things better.

He attempts to spend time alone with the kids. He bought me a mother's day out for Mother's Day, which will leave him alone with them. He plans my outing during their naptime, and I try to enjoy my time alone. I stare at my book before me, but it cannot hold my attention. My phone burns in my pocket, but I force myself not to call. I stare out the window of a small coffee shop, and I think of him. I wonder if he is okay.

I stay away only through naptime. They will be awake when I get home, but not for long. He craves this experience. He is testing himself. Since he hasn't called me for help, I assume they are all doing okay.

There is a look of pure joy on his face when I get home. He has proven he is still a father. He is still involved. He is still connected. I see pride again. I see confidence. I hug him. "See, you still got it," I whisper in his ear.

Amelia runs to me, and I meet David's eyes. He is happy. He holds Elijah and watches Amelia with loving eyes. "Mommy hold you!" she says, clawing my legs.

"Just a second, baby. Let Mommy put down her purse."

David's pride has made him more confident, more secure in his surroundings. "Come here, baby, and let Daddy hold you," he says.

"No! Don't like Daddy." There is complete silence.

"David? Honey? She doesn't mean it. She says she doesn't like a lot of things. She really doesn't mean it." I try to make him understand. He needs no help. He understands her truth more than anything. She is the only one not denying the truth.

"I know," he says quietly and walks away. He won't talk. He won't look. He won't listen.

Those few words of truth kill him like no war can. He is broken again. His shoulders slump. He tries to keep it all in. He tries to convince himself that it doesn't mean anything.

But it means everything to him. She has spoken his fear. She has given it life. His moment of triumph is over. He is a stranger again.

Demons

David is distant and almost cold. He is crawling in his own skin. I don't know how to comfort him. He doesn't know how to be comforted. I want to tell him I can take it all and that I can feel his pain for him. I want to see what he has seen so that he can erase it from his mind.

He is frigid and tense. He tries to pretend he is okay, but he pulls away from me when I try to hug him. He is eerily quiet. He takes deep breaths in some vain attempt to clear dust, debris, or stagnant air. He clutches his chest and cringes in pain from panic and fear of a force unseen. He reassures me that he is fine and that he is safe. He tells me no one will ever touch his sweet spot reserved only for his family.

He is lying. He is trying to protect me from something. Just days ago he was in a truck, driving through Baghdad looking for snipers, bombs, trained killers, and suicide bombers. Now he is in an SUV, trying to feel normal, safe, fatherly, husbandly, calm, and affectionate.

I want to help him. To take it all. To feel it all. He is evasive and short with me, yet completely giving to his children. He is secure with them because they can't read his actions or prod him with questions about what is happening to him. He cuddles with Amelia at night, reading her books and telling stories about magical fairies and unicorns. He rocks Elijah for hours. He traces the features of Elijah's face and kisses him gently on the forehead.

He is unpredictable. He weeps when something reminds him of how much his children have changed and forgotten so much about him. He revolts when he realizes how much he has missed with them. He is raging inside and seems out of control.

He covers my head and pushes me to the truck floor when the car behind us backfires. He speeds off, never looking back, and never explaining his actions. Another day, he beats the steering wheel with rage when he realizes he forgot to buckle Amelia into her seat.

"David, let me drive," I say, shocked by his outburst. He relents and stops the truck. I buckle Amelia in her seat, and attempt to calm him. He shakes and can hardly catch his breath. I ramble and stutter. "David, you're fine. . . . No problem. . . . We didn't even get out of the parking lot. . . . She let us know. . . . Please don't worry." I am worried.

"I should know better than that! You would think I have never been around kids!" He stews in his mistake the entire way home, while I sit in silence.

The explosions disappear as quickly as they ignite. He becomes quiet and melancholy. He is absent from any conversation. He talks to no friends and little family. He segregates himself from the rest of the world. His once vibrant and chatty phone calls have been replaced with monotone answers. He avoids the phone. He has no desire to initiate conversation and he avoids any and all topics surrounding the war.

He tells me he is in two different places and that he is trying to keep his sanity. He is trying to keep his morale high and to maintain his ability to survive over there. He is trying to stay cold. If he is cold, he can perform. If he is distant, he can go out every day and put his life on the line. If for one moment he melts, or gives in to relaxation and calmness, he may never be able to return to Iraq. Not mentally. He won't leave us if he lets himself feel. He won't come home in one piece if he lets down his guard.

How can he expect to come home and leave it all there for two weeks? How can I expect it?

It is a separate kind of torture. He cannot leave Iraq to be completely with us, and he cannot go back to Iraq without fresh memories of us to keep him going.

I refuse to be angry with him. I refuse to demand anything of him. I let him be cold, distant, and reserved. He needs to be. I laugh when he wants to laugh, and I force stillness in myself when he needs quiet.

Traces of him emerge when he is around his children. They melt his heart. He breathes them in as if their scent is the entire reason he exists. Because I know him, because I breathe him, I know they are his only truth and that we are all that matters in his world.

I push myself not to interrogate him. But, after a week of standing back, I finally beg him to tell me what it is that hurts. I want him to tell me what he has seen. I want to know. I need to know what has caused him to breathe differently.

"I can't tell you. You and the kids are the only pure things in my life," he says. "If I tell you what I have seen, what I have witnessed, what I have felt, then you will be tainted too. You will be touched by this same evil. I can't do that."

"But David, I want to help. You need to talk to someone." I beg him to tell me, to show me, or to give it to me. I plead with him to let me feel it with him. "I can't just sit back and watch this destroy you. Please, let me back in."

His blank eyes meet mine, and he holds my imploring stare. He takes one long deep breath. He speaks calmly and coldly. "We were called out on a mission one day to a mosque where a suicide bomber had killed seventy-two people." I feel him start to exhale while I inhale. It is coming into me. His pain is entering my body.

"When we got there, it had just happened. There was blood everywhere. So much blood. Blood like I have never seen. We were all standing in it. It was brown and muddy blood. They were pulling bodies out of the mosque and making sure that all of the people that were injured were being taken care of."

My mind starts to race. My God, I had seen this on the news online. I knew the name of the mosque. I can hardly breathe but force myself to lie still and stay silent.

"All around us were body parts. Hundreds of pieces were lying around. A foot here. A head there. Pieces of innocent people. It took me a moment to realize what I was standing on. I looked down and saw fingers, teeth, hair, and blood."

His voice is cold, distant, and calm. I am panicked. Tears sting my eyes. I lie in his arms and listen to his story, burning inside. My stomach lurches, and I feel myself convulsing beneath my skin. I try to maintain some sense of calmness. I will my body to stay still. I do not want him to stop. I want him to trust me. I don't want to appear afraid.

"The thing that really sticks out in my head is how much it didn't bother me. You always wonder how you are going to deal with things like that. What you are made of, ya know? I'm not sure what I am made of. But I do know that it changed me."

There is much more to tell, but his faraway trance is broken by my sobs. He looks at me with tender eyes and says, "See, I shouldn't have told you. I should have protected you." But he's wrong. I needed him to. I needed to help even if I didn't help. I needed him to be able to tell me. He holds me with tender arms. He is no longer distant and warmth returns to him. He starts to melt. I can see that I have created an avalanche. I almost wish I hadn't pushed him and pleaded with him to tell me. I think I can take this, but I'm not sure what it cost him. I watch him as each day passes, and we get closer to goodbye.

By the end of the two weeks, he is again resembling the loving, compassionate man I married, and I am grateful. But I am terrified by what I have done. He needs to put the cold, distant, calculated armor back on when he returns to Iraq because I need him to come home.

Crude Reality

I hate today. He is leaving again.

It is five in the morning, and I have to somehow prepare his little girl for another departure. David has been the one to greet her for two weeks. As we lie on the floor of the living room, avoiding all that today will bring, he rolls over and asks, "Would you mind getting her this morning?" I know he can't stand to hear her excitement that he is the one standing by her bed. I say nothing and go to wake her.

I open her door and allow a ray of light to spill into her room. She is sleeping soundly, contentedly, and Little Daddy is on the floor. He has not been in her bed for two weeks. She didn't need him.

"Mia. Wake up, baby." I nudge her softly and stroke her curly hair. She turns to me and the light in her eyes fizzles when she realizes I am the one waking her. "We have to take Daddy to the airport again. Daddy has to go back to work." She turns her eyes from me.

She stares at the wall while her fingers twirl the fuzzy tuft on her dolly's head. She sits up in the bed and pushes me out of her way. She crawls out of the bed and walks determinedly around the dark floor of her room. She peers under her bed and then crawls across the floor to look under her dresser. She looks back with panic on her face.

"What are you looking for?" I ask. She doesn't answer. She continues searching until her eyes fall on Little Daddy. She gently lifts him from the floor and pulls him close to her. She walks quietly through her door and out into the light of the hallway. I feel the familiar crack in my chest. She looks back into her room and asks with a dull, monotone voice, "Mommy, you coming?" I pull my shoulders back and take a deep breath. I follow her into the light of the hallway.

It is still dark outside when we take David to the airport. It is the same small airport with unfriendly faces. We ride silently in the truck. I don't know what to say. I'm afraid my voice will fail me if I speak. "Daddy going to work on big airplane?" Amelia asks quietly.

I choke. I can't answer. I don't want to answer. David looks out the window and remains silent. Finally I push the words from my chest. "Yes, baby. Daddy is going back to work. He will be home soon, okay?" I tell her with a happy, squeaky voice.

The first burst of morning spreads across the runway when we reach the airport. David is quiet. We watch him go through security. They nearly cavity-search him. How many soldiers going to Iraq are real security threats? They make him walk through the metal detector over and over. Each time, he has to remove one more piece of his issued uniform. It seems ridiculous. David is the one fighting a war that is supposedly to decrease the need for this kind of security. Other people walk through with no incident.

I stand inches from him. There is only a glass half-partition to separate us. I look at him over the glass and give in to my desire to touch him. I want to feel his fingers intertwined with mine. Just one last time.

"Ma'am you can't have any more contact with him," a stout man tells me from behind the glass.

"Are you kidding? I can't even reach over this to touch him? I can't hug him one last time? I can't let him hold his babies one last time?"

"No. You are not secure. We have no way of knowing that you won't hand him an illegal substance," he says coldly. I stare in disbelief.

David has to walk through security again because of my touch. He holds his tongue, and moves through the necessary steps. He sits on the secure side of the glass and takes turns making silly faces with Amelia. There is a small space beneath the glass. It is just big enough to fit her hand through. She finds it and touches his boot. David bends down, sticks his fingers under the partition, and tickles her hand. Her laughter brings attention to us again.

"I will not tell you again to keep your hands on this side. That is your last warning."

I hate him. "She is only two," I spit at him. He doesn't answer me. He meets my stare with equal determination. David says nothing. He doesn't want a scene. He doesn't want anger surrounding our goodbye. I am willing and ready to fight. He meets my eyes and silently begs me to let it go. I look away and try to calm myself.

They call for the passengers to board, and David turns to us one last time, making sure not to breach his security. I search for something to say. Something comforting. Something loving. Anything to ease this pain. "Please take care of yourself."

He meets my eyes and then immediately turns away. "I'll see you soon, babies. I love you. Take care of Mommy." He looks at me briefly and says, "I'll see you soon." He turns away and picks up his gear. I let him. We have learned by now that trying to extend a goodbye doesn't make it any easier.

David walks out. We watch him get on the plane. Amelia stands on a bench next to me, and she raises her tiny arms in protest. "No. Don't want Daddy airplane. No! Don't want it! Mommy, don't want it!" She screams at the tops of her lungs. She falls to her knees on the bench and convulses. There are no more words. She moans, then wails. I cry and hold her. She pushes against me and kicks my legs. She flails in my arms, and I hold her tighter.

She pulls back. She stares into my wet eyes with her wet eyes. Hers are full of contempt. They are twitching. She meets my gaze without blinking. She is sizing me up. She is daring me to tell her it is okay.

I want to tell her it isn't okay. She has every right to hate all this. I want to tell her to scream, kick, bite, punch, or destroy anything that would ever take her daddy away from her. But, if I load her with that ammunition, I am afraid I will destroy her. I have no choice. "It's okay," I tell her over and over again. "Daddy will be home soon." She stares at me. She is unmoving. She will not leave him.

I search for a way to ease her pain. I dig deep. "Want to go watch Daddy's plane take off?" Fun voice! Fun voice! Fun voice! Children need the fun voice! We are all having fun! Daddy is leaving, but we are really happy about it! Fun voice! Fun voice!

She responds slowly, climbing down from the bench and clutching Little Daddy to her chest. I smile at her. Inside, I am convulsing with agony. My steps are heavy. My heart is wild. My legs are twitching, and my eyes are blinded with tears.

We stand next to the truck and watch his plane fly overhead. She is silent. We stand there until his plane becomes part of the clouds. Somehow we have to leave.

I try to put her into the truck. She plants her feet firmly on the side of it. Her body starts to tremble. "No Mommy. No Mommy. I don't want it. I want Daddy. No Mommy. No Mommy. No Mommy! I don't want it!"

I bury my head in her hair and search for a way out. I don't want it either. "Wanna try to catch Daddy's plane?"

Her cries soften. "Yeah," she whispers. She has nothing left. No voice in this decision. No power to change it. No daddy to hold. And only me to trust. She relents. Her legs begin to give and her body starts to fold in on itself.

I put her in her seat. She looks for his plane. She cranes her neck around me. She is trembling, crying. With no plane in sight, and no fight left, she finally gives up. She is broken. But her voice is even when she speaks again. "Daddy go to work again."

Depression

"The mind is its own place, and in it self

Can make a Heav'n of Hell, a Hell of Heav'n."

—John Milton, *Paradise Lost*

Torture Chamber

David is gone. Again. I have to keep telling myself that he won't be there waiting for us when we go home. I look over into the seat next to me, and I see him. I hear him laughing when Amelia says something funny. I hear him whistling in the back of my mind.

I pull into our driveway, unload the kids from the truck, and walk into our empty, cold house. He envelopes me. His cologne lingers in the bathroom. His soap lounges in the shower. Behind my eyes, he stands in front of the mirror as he shaves. His laughter rings in my ears. His wet towel sulks on the floor, and the food that he didn't finish waits on the table.

Friends call me, trying to offer comfort. Family members call to offer support. I find myself comforting them as they cry for him. They want to help me, to be there for me, but there is nothing they can say. I lie: I tell them I am fine, that I will be fine, and that I am more concerned for Amelia. I tell everyone that we had a great two weeks and that everything was perfect.

It was almost worth it. While he was home, we had no phone calls, no bills, and no television. We stayed up until the wee hours of the morning. We had the greatest conversations of our marriage. We cuddled on our air mattress on the living room floor and talked about so many things. We listened to each other so intently. We held each other tighter than ever before. We walked closer. We talked quieter. And we didn't fight. Not once. But there were dark things circling us.

I wanted to argue. I wanted to talk about the huge things between us; the elephants in the room. We didn't dissect his anger. Didn't speak of my resentment. I didn't question his feelings about the war. We didn't try to analyze what hovered around us. We never discussed our future in the Army or how we would handle the next deployment. We left it all hanging in the air. With him gone again, the spell is broken. The weight of our issues is heavy and thick.

We had fourteen days to be together, only to be left alone again on day fifteen. I allowed myself to feel him again, to laugh again. I allowed tears to fall and offer me a small release. I allowed myself too much, and now this goodbye is more devastating than the first.

When he left the first time, I could only imagine what he faced. Now, I know in graphic detail what awaits him. And I knew what was waiting for me at home. These last two weeks have given us a glimpse of the life we are denied. We had a moment of happiness again, and now it has been stripped from our already raw hearts for the second time. This time I knew the emptiness that was there to meet me at the door. I dread returning to our computer marriage, to seeing Amelia and Elijah settle for a two-dimensional father once again.

Our first goodbye felt like a funeral. These two weeks were a joyous resurrection followed by a brutal massacre. The warnings of the other wives echo in my ears. They were right. It wasn't worth it. They weren't worth David's confusion and disorientation. They weren't worth watching my daughter scream, beg, and claw for him. They weren't worth the twisted knot in my chest. They weren't worth the return of the silence.

Before he came, we had a rhythm. We had a plan of attack for how we would endure this deployment. We had a routine and we were moving past the pain of losing him. Now, we have lost him again. Our rhythm has been obliterated. Our wounds have been reopened. Now, everything will be on my shoulders again. I am alone. And he is in misery, too.

I want to escape everything about this day. I sit on the couch, alone once again. The couch seems bigger. The house seems bigger. The world seems bigger.

I watch the kids play all day. Elijah is happy to be on the floor amusing himself with his toys. Amelia is confused. She plays happily for a while and then turns to me, almost seeming guilty, and says, "Daddy go to work again?"

I push through the day with false laughter. I talk of the weather and discuss life after the deployment, creating visions of vacations that we will all take together. Each new phone call is a deceitful descent into hopeless oblivion.

I put the kids to bed and lie on the couch with his shirt, the one he wore the day before. I wrap it around me and breathe in. I curl up with his shirt and long for him. I lie awake for hours and long for his thick hair. I miss his sweet smile. I crave his laughter. I imagine his body lying next to mine in our bed. I dream of his cologne. I listen for his whistle as he walks through the house.

I inhale, smell everything him, and wait for his return.

Nightmare

I sleep as little as possible. One constant dream taunts me and leaves me sweating and gasping for air. It always begins the same way, night after night.

In my dream, I wake up breathing easily, freely. It looks warm outside. Spring has finally emerged. I pull myself off the couch, and listen to my babies. They pull in deep breaths and exhale in small moans of deep content.

I put on the coffee and actually open the windows to allow the stagnant winter air to leave. Better things are coming. Elijah is awake, and he starts to play in his crib. I sit next to the monitor and listen to his giggles as he kicks the toys around. He is such a calm baby, and he rarely asks for anything.

I slowly open the door to get him. This is my favorite part of the day. It is the moment when I have missed them throughout the night and they are excited and surprised to see me. He is laughing when I walk in. He pushes his hips up into the air, begging for me to get him, to nuzzle him, and to hold him close and breathe him in.

I lift him high into the air, and his mouth opens. I pull him close to me and revel in the joy he pushes through my body. He makes me feel needed, unique, and brave. He giggles when I tickle his feet, and he nuzzles my neck as I carry him through the house. I put him in his saucer and pour him a cup of milk. He smiles happily and holds out his greedy, chubby hands.

Amelia begins to emerge from slumber. She always does so grudgingly, reluctantly, and angrily. She whines. It evolves from a tiny moan to a giant scream as she stretches and pushes her arms and legs into the new day. "Mommy hold you!" she yells from her bed.

I open her door with a broad smile, and she sits in the middle of her toddler bed. She extends out her delicate arms waiting for me to come get her. We cuddle next to her bed. She holds her dolly in her arms, playing with her tag, and twirling her fuzzy tuft in her fingers. It melts me. "Mommy loves to snuggle bunny with you," I tell her. She says nothing, only grunts her response. Little Daddy is next to her keeping watch.

I hold her until she is ready to face what the day has to offer. She wants to go outside to the Technicolor spring, and I am only too happy to agree with her. We are both ready to shake the winter from our bones.

I begin to make breakfast while my two beautiful babies play together on the living room floor. They are laughing. I know David will call soon, and we will be whole for those short ten minutes on the phone.

My reverie is interrupted. There is a knock on the door. I haven't even brushed my teeth; I have on my pajamas. It is too early for visiting friends, and the urgency of the knock alarms me.

I peek through the hole, but I only see a black beret, nothing more. I open the door, and my world stops. Standing at my front door are two soldiers in their dress uniforms. They are quiet. They are motionless. They are here for only one reason.

"Good morning, ma'am," one soldier begins, but I hear nothing he says. There is no blood in my body. I am cold all over. I can't feel. I can't think. I hate them immediately. I know why they are here. They are death calling.

My feet are cold. My whole body feels wet. I turn to the side of the door and slowly start to slide down the wall. I feel myself vomit. I am not sure if I hear them, or if I am imagining what they are saying. I hear a dull buzz in my head.

"Is there anything we can do? Anyone we can call for you?" Their voices are dull and monotone. I hate them. I am walking in a house of black. There is no color anymore. I feel myself being picked up and walked to the couch. I see one of them holding my daughter. I cannot feel her. I am dead. Gone.

The dream ends in nothingness. I sit straight up on the couch and hear the monitor scanning through the channels. Both kids are sleeping soundly. All is quiet. It is dark. The living room clock ticks and the abandoned television buzzes. I can't breathe. I am wet, cold, and shaking. I tell myself over and over again that it is just a dream.

I walk to the kitchen, unsure of myself. The microwave clock reads three thirty-five. I pour myself a glass of water and try to calm my raging heart. I try to breathe evenly, to focus on the blue numbers of the clock as I hold the heavy glass in my shaking hands. I sip from it as slowly as I can. It is just a dream. Just a dream. Please, God, let it just be a dream.

I walk into Amelia's room and watch her sleep. I sit on the floor next to her bed and listen to her snore, watching her chest rise and fall.

Just a dream. I open the door to Elijah's room. He is on his belly with his feet curled under him in the fetal position. I climb onto my bed and mimic him, crying into the pillow.

Just a dream. It is nearly dawn. I can't sleep. I walk through our hallway and stare at all the pictures capturing our life together. David is always smiling. He is always laughing. He is always open. His spirit is easily captured on film. I pull one from the wall, the one of him holding his babies, and I clutch it to my chest. New tears fall as I recreate the day in my head. Me, laughing and snapping pictures. Him, holding his newborn and his pink-clad toddler.

I sit on the couch for hours waiting for the phone to ring. My body refuses to function until I know he is all right. The kids are awake and playing. I am trying to find the will to play, to laugh, and to exist outside my fear. I am trying to emerge outside my head and heart.

I move through the morning of diapers, potty training, and begging Elijah for just one more month of nursing against his growing will. The minutes tick by with no compassion. It is late afternoon before I hear his voice, and breathe again. My mind begins to let go of the fear and anxiety. He tells me he was out on a mission.

"I had the dream again last night," I whisper into the phone. There is only silence on the other end. I hate myself that I have made him think of it, but I only have him to talk to about these fears. We only have each other. He is the only other person in the world who can understand the fear that I have of life without him.

"Don't worry, baby. It was just a dream. Everything is fine." I hear the uncertainty in his voice, and I choose to ignore it. I take in the false security he is offering, and I breathe.

Haunted

Today is Memorial Day, a day of hamburgers and barbecue. I think back to images of graduation hats flying through the air, clear dusky skies filled with lightning bugs, and the smell of freshly cut grass. I remember the sensation of chilly water lapping against my legs as I dangled them over the dock's edge, the aroma of impending summer, and having butterflies in my stomach at the thought of summer romance.

I think, now, of those smells, those intoxicating smells, and I wonder what smell is filling David's nose today. Does he smell burnt flesh, gunpowder, gasoline?

I think of the joy of riding on a boat and feeling the wind tangling my hair. Feeling and hearing the sloshing waves against the fiberglass siding.

Is David in his armored truck, moving through Baghdad with his helmet and goggles on, his bulletproof vest weighing on his shoulders? He says the equipment is suffocating, heavy, and hot.

I think of family gatherings that celebrated the arrival of summer. We are all happy and laughing, thinking of no school, lighter work, and sleeping late. Hearty hands clap backs and thick arms hug and hold babies while the intoxicating smells of cooking food fill the sultry air.

Is David looking back, too? Wishing he were in college again, waiting for the chance to voice his opinion or ride his bike across campus. Stopping to climb trees and do his homework from a heightened perspective.

My mind fills with memories of the times that my mother and father took me to the cemetery. I stand in the tall grass and wish the time away. My father, standing next to a grave, wipes a tear from his face. It was the grave of a fallen friend. My father served in Vietnam, and he lost many friends there in those jungles. When he brought me with him to pay respect, I looked the other way and silently begged him to hurry home to get our boat in the water.

Memorial Day used to be about men before my time. Now, there are men and women years younger than I am dying every day. I see them more clearly now. Their sacrifices and bravery. I can see the mother kissing her babies goodbye. The father walking away from his teenage son. The sister telling her brother she will return. The brother asking his little brother to take care of the family. The aunt explaining to her nephew why she has to go away. The uncle sending letters to his niece. The son waiting in line to call his mother. The daughter e-mailing loving words to her father. The friend standing over a wounded soldier. The lover waiting for a letter to come. Now, I see them as people. Not as nameless soldiers. And not as stenciled letters on a tombstone.

I feel the fringe of summer now, and welcome it. But not without looking back. I know I will begin to inhale those familiar smells again. The barbecue. The chlorine. The honeysuckle and watermelon.

Those will always fill my nose. But the new smell of freshly dug dirt will keep those aromas from smelling as sweet.

Shackled

Knowledge does not free me. It enslaves me. I can only be free when the news is not on. I can only exist when magical children's music oozes out of the television, radio, and truck speakers.

I tried to watch the news during the first deployment. I listened to every press conference covering the war in Afghanistan. I thought a good Army wife needed to. I tried to understand the intent of the president. To listen to and respect world leaders with my husband's life in their hands. I tried to listen and attempted to watch.

With endless information streaming across the television screen, I had to keep from imagining David's name moving across the bottom in tiny bold-faced type. I had to try to keep from seeing his picture flash on the television and to avoid believing everything that they said to me. Men and women spoke of names, units, deaths, and widows in the same breath that they spoke of celebrities, of cats in trees, and protestors. I tried to know the names of all that had fallen and forced myself to listen, observe, and weed through the information. "Two Fort Drum soldiers killed today in combat. More at six." Next subject.

I was hoping to understand and be involved with David's life over there. No amount of media coverage could help. When David once called at three in the morning, he said, "I am okay. So, whatever you see on the news didn't involve me." I watched but didn't see anything on the news. Some celebrity marriage was more important.

I tried. Because I tried last time, I try to escape this time. But images of men fighting, men that could be David, are all over the television. They invade my fluffy television shows. I keep the television off through the day. Amelia isn't allowed to watch. She only has videos. The breaking news coverage and snippets of war aren't just random images for her. In her world, they are pictures and media feeds of her daddy running, shooting, or exploding.

I turn to my computer, but images of war infiltrate the screen when I check my e-mail, and I cannot get away from them. When they are there, in front of me, I cannot keep myself from staring at the screen, trying to see his face, always hoping that I will not see his face. Army policy is to tell me before the media if he gets hurt, but there is always room for mistakes.

I hear snippets on the radio. Key words are on the television at night. "Iraq" is everywhere on the Internet news. My heart jumps with fear as small glimpses of stories catch my attention and hold me captive. "Another suicide bombing in Baghdad." "Car explodes in Baghdad." "More Fort Drum soldiers killed in Baghdad." I always want more. And then am terrified when I hear more. There is no escaping it.

I cannot watch the news. If I turn it on, for days I'll become addicted to the screen. I'll beg them to show me more. The more I see, the more I can look for his face. The more I look, the more I can try to make sure that he is safe.

There is no avoiding it. People send me e-mails that are meant to boost morale or to show how the soldiers are living or to remind the public that they are still there. I guess they want me to know that they remember. But I don't want to be reminded that they could ever forget. They are sent in good faith, and I know there is a shred of me that they see in these e-mails. I understand they are thinking of me, but I cannot read them. I delete them. Pictures of fathers reading letters from tiny hands and wives sleeping next to the caskets of their husbands don't make me feel loved or remembered. They only bring new painful images to my already filled brain.

The only news I want is his phone call. He doesn't talk about the violence. He doesn't talk about his missions. He doesn't talk about anything but his family. He needs to not be the news. We never discuss the war. We are happy on the phone. We are perfectly mannered. We all are living in a bubble of self-defense. This bubble keeps me free. It is a bubble that I choose. I don't want to discuss what could happen to us.

Collapsing

David left us a few weeks ago, and Amelia is having nightmares. She is having long, sweaty, heart-pounding nightmares. She is crying for David. And I have no way to help her.

"My Daddy! My Daddy! Want my Daddy!" she screams. I go to her room and hold her. She shakes and her hair hangs in sweaty ringlets. I try talking to her. "Daddy is at work, baby, but he loves you and misses you." I try to comfort her. She won't let me. I don't know what else to tell her.

Her tears wet my face. I hold her trembling body and comb my fingers through her wet hair. She pushes my hands away. "Don't," she says. I obey. She gets out of bed and runs to the front door, sobbing. "My Daddy home again."

I sit next to her on the cold floor by the door. I try to hold her, but she doesn't want me. She pushes me away. "No. Don't want you. Want Daddy." I try not to be offended, to focus what is left of my energy on her. I need to be calm for her.

She stands there weeping for an hour. She wails, and hits, and screams, and begs me to bring him back. She looks at me with hatred. She glares at me with anguish. I can only meet her stare with respect. I have no answers to give her. I sit next to her and let her cry, let it fall onto the floor and vanish into the concrete tile.

When she has nothing left in her, she falls into the floor in front of me. She is exhausted. Her eyes are full of anguish. Her body is limp. I pull her to me and lift her into my arms. Her neck is sweaty. I taste the salt on her cheek. She grips me. She holds me like she doesn't have any other choice.

"Want to sleep with Mommy?" I ask, stroking her tiny back.

"No. Want my bed." I walk her into her room, holding her, kissing her, and trying to find some way to take it away. I put her into bed. I sing to her. Tickle her. Kiss her. Hug her. Talk to her. Read her stories. I sit next to her until her breathing becomes normal and rhythmic. She is asleep again. I lie on the couch, and I listen for her tiny, tortured voice through the night.

Raging Bulls

Amelia and I are constantly angry and frustrated with each other these days. It's almost as if we're competing for the right to miss David the most. I want to tell her he belonged to me first and that she doesn't have the right to be so angry. She yells at me, and I fight and cringe not to scream at her. She tells me to leave her alone, and I retaliate. She is two, and I am twenty-nine. That should make a difference. It should matter to me. But it doesn't. I resent her for venting her frustrations. I want to yell in anger, cry at random. I want to hit, punch, and kick and scream. But I don't. And so we fight. And fight. And fight. And then love. And love. And love.

She is so much like me. Her temper is vibrant, and she sees in David all that is peaceful and calm. He settles her. And his serene nature tames me. She misses him just as much as I do. I can feel every nerve ending standing on edge when I hold her. They mirror mine. She is mourning him.

For that reason, we are not a good pair. I want to tell her to deal with it, to quit wallowing in her own misery. I want her to leave me alone so that I can wallow in mine. My pity party is selective. She isn't invited.

My reality is tortured and my sense of compassion and understanding has been chiseled away since he left. I want to remember that she is only a child and she needs me. I want to tell her that all will be fine and that he will be home soon. He will play with her again, the way that she is yearning for him to. I want to tell her not to worry, not to cry, not to ask for him, and not to miss him. It will all be over soon.

I want to believe it. There are constant circling rumors that they will be home soon. I also hear I should expect another six months. We have no idea when he will come home, and only Amelia gets to act angry and frustrated.

I try to be patient with her anger, with her emotions, her needs, but they are eating me alive. I want to smack her, to yell at her. I want to tell her to shut up. I want to scream at her, to use her as a punching bag the way that she uses me. I want to bite her back when she bites me. To smack her back when she hits me. I want to be her.

Instead, I stand by her. There is no one who can better understand my pain and hurt than she. She is two. And I am twenty-nine.

Dangling

I am at the end of my rope, dangling, and my sanity is breaking and scattering. Amelia continues to rage. "Daddy home!" she screams at the top of her lungs.

"I know, honey. Some daddies have different jobs. Daddy has to leave sometimes, but he will be home soon." I am tired of telling her. I don't believe it when I say it.

"Daddy home! Daddy home! Daddy home!" She continues to scream. She screams for hours every day. She stands on her toes to shout at me. "Daddy!" "Give me Daddy!" "I want Daddy!" "Daddy now!" She follows me, shrieking. She hits my legs with her tiny fists, yelling. She bangs her head in angered fits. She slams her forehead into the hard floor, the dining room table, and the wall; anywhere she can transfer some of her rage. I try to stop her, but there is little I can do. I hold her, letting her bang her head on my legs, my arms, and my shoulders. I take as much as I can in order to protect her from herself. Nothing calms her.

And her screeching voice makes every nerve in my body rise to the very edge of my skin and burn. I want to pull out every hair I have on my head. I try reasoning and singing. I try punishing and taking toys. I try talking. I try listening. Nothing works.

I search my addled mind for a happy place. There has to be something that will calm me and something that will help her. But I have no idea what that could be. With no clue how to stop it, I try to ignore it, to deter the shaking and convulsing. I try to find some way to help her release it.

"Don't want you. Want Daddy. Don't want you. Want Daddy." Over and over again. Perhaps it does comfort her. Maybe I should go outside and scream, "I want my husband" a million times in the most searing voice. Maybe that will help me. I don't try it. I don't have the guts to verbalize it. My mind runs in endless circles. Why won't she stop crying? Why won't she stop screaming? Why can't this ever be David's problem?

I stand in the hallway and listen to her in her bed. She has had very little to eat and she has refused to sleep for the past thirty-four hours. She has staged her own personal revolt. I am thankful, at least, that Elijah is capable of sleeping through her tirade.

She wails. And screams. And kicks the wall. I shrink to the floor and beg God to help me. I beg Him to give me the strength not to lose my patience, not to lose to my temper, or my resolve to hold this family together.

I pull my hair. I weep into the floor, into the only place that cannot mirror my pain. I bang my head repeatedly into the hard linoleum, and my mouth forms the words, "Please, God, please take this agony and frustration from me. Please, God, take it from me," over and over again.

I feel myself rising. Walking to her door is automatic and robotic. I am completely controlled by my emotions, and I have no idea what awaits me in hers. I touch her doorknob, not sure of what I am about to do. Not sure of what I will say or how I will respond to her defiance and anger. I am not sure if I will ever forgive myself for what is boiling inside me. I am unsure of my arms. Will they hurt her? I am unsure of my voice. Will I yell? I am terrified of what is consuming me.

I am met with silence. She is finally quiet. She is finally sleeping. The rage hisses from my body, and I return to the living room, searching my mind for some way to end it all.

Trial Separation

Today is our anniversary. We have been married for forty-eight months. He has been gone for twenty of them.

I stood barefoot beneath a tree four years ago and tugged softly on the long goatee falling from his chin. We were ready to move to Montana where I would teach, and he would hug trees and find new ways to clean our air. I floated in his arms while we danced to "I Got You Babe," and we both doubled over with laughter with cake in our hair and on our faces. That day was flawless.

Today is just another day. It is another day to get through. It is another day to put behind me. It is another day to wish away until he comes home. But it drags on and on. It feels as though it will never end.

The sounds of my playing children seem far away and lost. I am a fragment of that woman in white standing underneath a beautiful sycamore tree the day that began our life together. We stood before each other with such naïve ideas of how our life would be. We had lofty aspirations of how our marriage would transcend all marriages before it. We had dreams of how we would be as people, parents, and companions.

I knew on that day that I would love him forever. I swore to cherish him for the rest of my life. We tied our hands together to solidify that promise. We each sipped from a Cherokee drinking gourd and then smashed it to ensure that each day would be conquered together.

I know today that I love him past forever and that I cherish his smell, his kiss, his smile, his laugh, his beautiful black hair, his fingernails, the way he dances from foot to foot when trying to stand still, his desire always to make me happy, and his ability always to voice that desire. I miss his absent goatee, his smooth face, and the environmentalist that still exists beneath his Army uniform. I miss every tiny detail of him.

To say that I miss him sounds trite. To say that I miss him puts him in a category with home cooking, southern breezes, and big skies in Montana. I miss all those things. But I grieve for him. I am short of breath for him. He is all that I have come to know as true. He is the best part of me.

That part will not be filled by his call today. He is on a mission, and I know I will not hear from him. We are thousands of miles apart, and I can only imagine that he is trying to avoid thinking of all that today represents. He has to be pushing memories and everything about us from his mind in order to stay safe. Today is our anniversary.

Longing

I keep hearing from faceless voices that I am doing a good job, and that being a stay-at-home mother and Army wife is the most important job there is. But it doesn't feel important. It feels suffocating and unappreciated. It feels like my identity is gone, and my strong sense of independent womanhood is secondary to all that David is doing, all that he is going through, and all that he represents. I feel like a maid, a nanny, a chauffeur, a doormat, a punching bag, or an ant. My mind, my sense of purpose and my identity before all this are leaving me.

Working mothers and friends talk about being jealous of my ability to stay home with the kids, and I am thankful for being here to witness their expanding vocabularies and abilities. Only I notice the small things, the new moments of clarity in them. Only I see the exact moment when they finally get it.

Their growing minds are breathtaking to behold, and they do offer a great sense of accomplishment, but I miss the feeling of stepping out into the world and earning a paycheck for myself. I miss the feeling of knowing, rather than hoping, that I am making a difference. I miss putting on nice clothes and high heels. I miss being known for what I have accomplished for myself rather than for what I am now doing in relation to David's world.

I try to forget about it all and just move through and delve into the day with my children, feeling their excitement as they claw through dirt, or cheering and laughing with them as they experiment with paint on the walls. But that seems impossible when I know I am the one with the responsibility of disciplining and cleaning in their wake. The desire to be more burns inside me. I am more than that label: mother and wife. I am independent of it. I have two degrees, and I existed long before David or before the Army or even my children. I want to discuss more things than this war, my kids' play dates, or my husband's rank in the Army. But I have no way to voice that desire without feeling guilty. David is the one at war. I shouldn't be considering myself.

When people ask me how David is doing, I have a standard answer. "He is doing okay. He has had a rough year, but he is all right. He just can't wait to come home and see these babies."

And that is true. But what I really want to say is, "What about me? What about Amelia and Elijah?" I feel forgotten and unnecessary. To admit this makes me feel selfish. David's situation is the one that should be important. His struggle is more important.

I would never tell anyone that I don't feel important or admit the fear that my feelings don't seem to matter. I would never speak of the waning support for us left behind. I feel forgotten by the world. The war is a hot topic, but the faces that flash on the screen are images of media personalities rather than someone's husband, wife, son, or daughter. The story of the individual is lumped into the bustle of the war.

It makes me wonder why one face is more media-worthy than another. Why one Army wife is more special than the next. For one face on the television or in a newspaper, there are thousands left faceless and voiceless. And each Army wife is, first and foremost, a woman before she falls neatly into a category. Independent of those waiting for her support or of those clinging to her breast for nourishment.

But we are here. Trying to make it through every day. Forcing ourselves to put our children, spouses, and this war before our needs of individuality and respect. We are here, begging God to help us get up and praying we do not get sick so that we can continue to take care of our children, our husbands, our houses, and our continuous bills. Managing our cash flow, and ensuring each day is filled with education, healthy choices, and individual attention. We are here, honing our strength and pushing our children to understand, to listen, to accept, and to help in the fight to hold a household together. We are here, trudging through snow, shoveling it, driving through it, to make it to the doctor, the dentist, the play dates, gymnastics, school, and the emergency room. We are here, making sure every house functions, every child is fed, and every body is clothed.

We cannot allow our feelings of invisibility to stop us from being the mentor, the backbone, the tutor, the bather, the nurturer, the provider, and the punching bag of our families. We cannot allow this need to be fulfilled or even force ourselves to speak of it, nor can we admit we need to feel acknowledged. To do so would be to admit that we may be thinking of more than the needs of our spouses at war.

The weeks drag on and on with no end in sight, and I fight to understand my own needs. I talk to friends here who are going through the same thing. We're all too scared to cry. A moment of weakness might make it impossible to go on. We allow long silences on the phone. We can't even complain. To talk about our own need for acceptance and individuality seems toxic and indulgent. So I push the need to exist outside of this situation deep inside. But it doesn't work. And no one can understand but the Army wife next to me.

When I talk to friends and family who are further from this deployment, I pretend to listen about movies, car trouble, boyfriend trouble, husband trouble, and career issues. It all feels removed and foreign and insignificant to me. And that angers me, too. I can't submerge myself into the Army world, or I will feel lost, overlooked, and labeled and identified by everything David. When I do exist within the confines of the base, it angers me that I have no existence without David's approval.

I am defined by my husband's rank, his job, and his presence. I have to quote his social security number at the Army clinic. I have to show an identification card with his information just to enter the base. I have to show that card to prove I am his spouse in order to buy groceries. Where I can live on base is determined by his rank. I need his social security number to get medication. I need it to identify his kids. To take our cats to the vet. His social security number is imprinted on my brain. Mine is fading into the background. My identity is dwindling and nonexistent.

But I can't identify with anything that exists outside the Army, either. I have no sense of how it feels to walk the unemployment line. I can't relate to the failing economy. I have no concept of health insurance pains, and I hate that I can no longer casually identify with anything outside the Army gates. I feel lost and abandoned without any real sense of who I have become or what role I am meant to play.

I sit on the phone with my closest friend, and I try to focus on her issues. I want to hear her. To be her friend. But the weight of my burden will not allow it. "I wish I had your problem!" I finally snap. "My husband is at war while you complain about your husband not doing the dishes." I heave with sobs. And then realize the silence on the other end is one of shock. I am instantly ashamed. She has only intended to involve me in her life. But her life feels foreign, and I resent that I can no longer identify with her. I want to. I miss being in her shoes.

"I'm so sorry. That was uncalled for and completely insensitive. It isn't your fault. None of it is. I'm so sorry." I try to coax her into telling her story again, to convince her that this time I will be the friend I once was to her. She forgives me, but she dismisses the story as irrelevant. I hate myself for diminishing her.

I hang up the phone and try to forgive myself for snapping. I feel disgusting and repulsive. I have forgotten how to be decent to the very people who love and support me. I can only hope that they will understand and try to forget this moment in my life. I hope they realize I am not this insane. I am not this uncaring. I am not this selfish.

I hope I realize it. I hope that someday I can forget these feelings of resentment and that I can feel proud of the choices I made for myself and this family.

I lie on the couch and curl my legs to my chest. I hardly recognize myself anymore. I turn on the television and catch the end of a slapstick comedy. I catch myself berating it in my mind. How could this kind of stuff exist while there is a war going on? And then, I sigh with relief that this kind of stuff exists while there is a war going on.

Implosion

With all that's going on in the world, it's finally something so domestic, so primal, that undoes me. It's my son's dirty diaper. It beckons me. It is all too familiar. It is all that I do. It is all that I smell. It is all consuming. He plays happily in his saucer while the smell taunts me and mocks me.

I put him on the bed and begin to take off his diaper, all the while talking on the phone to a friend. My fingers touch something hot. Something slimy. Elijah's leg is covered in poop. Slathered. I look down onto my arm and hip, and there it is, staring, teasing, and laughing at me. I am covered in poop, too. It is all over my bed. All over my arm. It is all over Elijah. It is everywhere. He laughs and grunts and giggles.

I grab a towel from the laundry waiting to be folded. I put him on it, and attempt to clean him. Panic brews in me. My heart pounds and my chest heaves. I tell my friend I have to go and hang up the phone. I can't breathe.

I go through the motions until he is clean, with a new diaper, in the crib. I wonder what I should do with his clothes, the bedspread, my clothes, and his saucer. I walk into the living room, and there is poop under the saucer and on it. Everything is spinning. The room is closing in, and I can hear a ringing in my head.

It all has to be thrown out. Everything has to leave the house. That is the only way to regain control. That is the only way that my home can be clean again. This revelation allows me to breathe again. I can think clearly, and I begin to steady myself in the room. Everything feels okay again.

Until I look down and see brown footprints on the floor. I stepped in it. Behind me, there are footprints leading to my room. They lead to the diaper and to Elijah.

The room closes. A snapping sound fills my head. Everything is black. Then white. Then black. Elijah cries in his crib. I am frozen. I can't walk because I will continue to spread it. I can't take off my shoes because the floor is dirty. I can't move. There is no alternative but to stand here until David can help me. I can't move until he is home. He can clean everything around me.

My mind explodes. I am dirty, full of filth. Toxic. I am illuminating filth. My hands feel like they are crawling. It feels like tiny bugs are eating my flesh. My hair stands on end. I am cold all over.

The whole room spins in slow motion while my heart races and bulges in my chest. I am paralyzed, but Elijah falls asleep. Amelia is working on a puzzle and listening to music. She is eating a snack and happily humming along. My body refuses to move. Not until David gets home and he cleans.

I look from one footprint to the next. I begin to wonder where I have walked. Which part of the floor will ever be clean again? Will the stain ever leave? Amelia and Elijah can never walk on this floor again either. My throat is closing, and I can see my heart pounding inside my chest. My little circle is the only safe place in the house. If I never move, I can contain it. Everything is spinning, and I am panicking. I feel trapped in my own head. I imagine scenarios of parasites and viruses plaguing my family because nothing will ever be clean again.

With no one to help me, I could stand here and avoid all of this until he comes home. I could stand here for months. It seems rational to me. It seems plausible. I could wait here for an eternity if it meant not having to face the insanity that is brewing in my body.

"Mommy. I finished." I hear her voice in what seems like a tunnel. I am thankful for it. I have to do something. I can't crack right in front of her. There has to be some way out of this. Everything feels dirty. My life. My house. The base. The war. This deployment. It is all dirty. I am repulsed by it, and I want to walk out and search for a place that is pure. I could remove myself from all that surrounds me and disappear. I want to pack them up and take them with me to somewhere warm and inviting.

"Mommy!" I push myself to do something, anything to keep my mind from running away with my will. I want to keep myself strong. My kids can't watch me unfold. My arms raise over my head; my body is fighting my brain. My shirt moves over my head and falls to the floor. I refuse to crumble. "Just a second, baby. Mommy needs a minute," I tell her from somewhere in my brain. She seems satisfied with my answer, and she drops her empty bowl on the floor beside her. She moves on to the toys surrounding her.

I become more agitated and bend down to remove my shoes. I can only walk into the kitchen. It is the one place in the house that I know I haven't been. I throw away the shirt and the shoes and search through the kitchen cabinets until I find an old container of bleach. I begin a slow journey through the house, crawling on the floor and cleaning with bleach and several towels.

I make it to Elijah's room and clean his floor. With the sharp smell burning my nose, I can stand and attempt to tackle the bedspread, his clothes, the towel, and his diaper.

Everything has to be thrown away. If I wash his clothes and then wash the towel, then the washer will be dirty. When I dry the clothes and the towel, the dryer will be dirty. Every piece of clothing after that will always be dirty. There is no other way. I have to throw away all of it. I need to throw away my shirt, the shoes, Elijah's clothes, the bedspread, the towel, and the sheets. I tie it all up in a garbage bag and put it outside, far away from me.

183

I feel dirty, crazy, repulsed, and terrified. I search for the phone, and hide in the bathroom. I sit on the edge of the tub and try to slow my breathing by rocking back and forth. The swaying motion feels graceful, and it calms me.

The phone rings. It is David. I don't want to stop rocking to answer. Sitting on the bathtub, I feel peaceful. I push myself to stop moving as his voice comes through the phone. Elijah is still sleeping, and Amelia is now playing in her room across from the bathroom.

"Hey," I hear him say. All I can do is cry. Slowly, I begin to tell him what happened. I wait for him to tell me that I am insane and that I need to be put away somewhere. At this point, I would agree with him. It is all irrational. It is all unnecessary. I have no idea why such a simple situation could make me feel completely powerless and insane.

Instead I hear, "You're fine. You just have too much going on. I feel the same way sometimes. Just like you are going to go insane if you don't have some way to release the pain." I begin to weep, and I tell him every bit of fear that is circling my brain. I whimper.

"I don't feel clean, David. I have washed my hands a million times. They are raw and cracking. I don't know what to do. I don't think I can hold the babies because I feel so disgusting." I sob and begin rocking again.

"You're fine. I promise it is all okay." I try to believe him. Elijah is awake, and he stirs in his crib. He begins to cry, and I am petrified. I am afraid my craziness will somehow jump from my skin to his. I am afraid I will taint him. I am terrified that my insanity will somehow creep through my hands and destroy him.

"I hear him crying, honey. I need you to go to him and pick him up," he tells me. "You won't let your baby cry. I know that you won't."

"I can't, David," I whimper.

He is more forceful this time. "Get up and walk into that room. I know you have it in you. Your son needs you."

I walk timidly into his room. I stand over his crib. He is smiling at me, and he is holding up his arms, asking for me. I look away, hiding from him. "I can't, David. I feel insane. I feel like I will make him crazy if I touch him. I feel completely out of my mind insane. This wouldn't have gotten to a normal person."

"It would get to anyone. Now pick up Elijah for me. I need you to." I bend down to get him, begging my hands to touch him. "Melissa, pick up our son." I listen and do as I am told.

His skin is creamy. His smile is innocent. He laughs. He instantly calms me. I look into his crystal eyes, and I am swaying again. His toothless grin is infectious. I am lost in him. David's voice is somewhere in the distance.

"There you go. See? You're not crazy. It's just all too much," he explains. "You have to crack at some point. That was it. It is all over now. You won't crack again."

"How do you know that, David?" I ask.

"Because I can hear you breathing again. I can hear him laughing. And I know you. Feel better?" he asks.

"Yeah, I do. Do you think I am crazy? Do you think that I need treatment or something?"

"No, baby. You're not crazy," he whispers. I feel calm, steady.

"I'm really embarrassed, David. I would die if anyone knew what just happened." I stop myself, and then continue. "I just felt so dirty and gross."

"Don't worry, baby. We all lose it sometimes." Our ten minutes are over.

Acceptance

"Together they waged a perfunctory

battle against the outrageous

behavior of that place. . . .

For they understood the source of

the outrage as well as they knew

the source of light."

—Toni Morrison, *Beloved*

Dusting My Cobwebs

My fists are unclenched, and I have pulled myself from the floor. I cannot berate, degrade, or shame what I cannot change. This is our life. David is gone. I am here with two beautiful children. I have no choice but to see the truth of it. No amount of anger can bring him back. No amount of depression can will him home.

Finally, there is a release within me. I find comfort in my solitude and calming peace in the quiet of my house. I have finally turned off the noise and learned to face the silence. I no longer wish to fool myself. He isn't here. And he won't be here tomorrow. I am all that is left, and I do not mind being alone. It has never been that.

I do not mind the time to myself at night. I think about my future, my career paths, my goals, and my mental well-being. I think about writing again and about what I want to be as a mother, as a wife, and as a woman. I toy with the idea of going back to school again. I think about life without fear, without war, and without tears. I talk to God without yelling at Him. I am quiet now, finally listening for an answer.

Winter has finally released its grip on us. I sit outside with the baby monitor and watch the world around me. I take the time to inhale the scent of pine and listen to the trees bending and pleading with the wind. Birds are finally emerging.

I take the time to work on my body, exercise, and listen to my joints. I stretch them and pull them with yoga. I breathe and radiate. I relax with long, hot baths and lather myself with lotion. I read books with pure joy and focus on cultivating my mind.

It is not being alone that burns my spirit. It is the loneliness. It is what is missing. I searched for David for twenty-five years. I spent so much time grooming myself for a perfect mate. I prepared my heart, questioned my existence, and primed myself for a relationship. I learned to give to another person, learned to share a life with someone. I learned to listen wholly and willfully. I learned how to say, "I'm sorry," and, "I was wrong." It took a long time to learn these lessons. And I have had very little time to use them.

I have always enjoyed being alone. I still do. I relish the time to think and expand. To consider all that I am. To question and explore.

But, I don't enjoy being without the one who has caused life to smell more delicious. I inhale his fading scent in the house and remember the laughter and easy smiles. I hold his shirts at night, like Penelope awaiting Odysseus, and I dream of family vacations and dinners around the table. Those memories will live again someday. Hopefully.

For now, I pass time with friends, put my children in fun activities, and groom myself again, this time for his return. I am a member of the support group. I reach out to my neighbor. I laugh with friends and share stories of my children. I attend welfare functions, and call upon another spouse when needed.

I appreciate all of the support that they offer. But I still sleep alone. Support groups and friends can't touch my face and cause my heart to pound. No amount of companionship or alone time will ever compare to the emptiness without him.

Pinky Toes and Butterfly Kisses

There are days when Amelia and Elijah can melt the coldness of this desolate place. She is beautiful. She is clean, playing with bubbles in the bath and washing her feet with infectious laughter. She is dirty, running to me with black earth in her teeth, showing me her new pet worm, squealing with delight. She is elegant in her pink "tutus" and her "glass" slippers. She is evolving into something that I never quite imagined.

She runs and plays like a kid now instead of a baby. She utters things that only David and I would find funny. She twists her words around. She adds consonants. She refers to herself as "Mommy's best girlfriend."

I watch her learn as she explores her world, and I can see her mind churning, see it developing and evolving. She repeats things that she hears me say. She is now a parrot with an ever-increasing vocabulary. Her hair is longer. I can put it into ponytails. When David left, she had very little hair. Her feet have grown three sizes. Her eyes are brighter, her belly is smaller, her cheeks are thinner, and her teeth are whiter.

When David left, Elijah was still a newborn. He had no idea that he even had hands or feet. Now he reaches, grabs, delicately touches. He stands tall in his saucer and repeatedly tries to "start" it with his plastic keys. He babbles constantly and curls his toes with glee as he hears his voice moving through high and low pitches.

His eyes sparkle and twinkle when he is about to smile. Happiness explodes from his eyes to his mouth. He knows some secret that he is bursting to tell. He doesn't respond to his name. His sister calls him "Bubby," and that is what catches his ears. She captivates him. He watches her run, jump, and play, envying all she can do.

David watches him grow on the web cam. He attempts to catch his tiny movements, but the web cam is slow and it only catches jerky motions. He relies on my play-by-play commentary. "Can you see him bouncing?" I ask the computer screen.

"No, but I can hear the saucer moving," David says.

"Sometimes he bounces so hard that he makes the saucer move across the floor!"

Amelia pushes her face into the view of the web cam. "Watch me, Daddy," she pleads. She jumps and twirls for him. The web cam only catches glimpses of her. "See me?" she asks.

"Of course, baby," he says. She runs back and forth in front of the web cam, always demanding that David keep his eyes on her. Elijah's eyes are riveted. David laughs, and I giggle while we watch our children. Together.

Through Her Eyes

Amelia calls all men in uniform "daddies." She is nearly obsessed with them. At first I thought it was sweet. I encouraged it. Now, I can't escape it. We are living on a base full of daddies always walking around, getting ready to deploy, or coming home from a deployment. They all have that same uniform. It spells dread and sadness for me.

Amelia loves that uniform. "Look at those daddies," she says when we walk into a building on base. "That daddy walking. That daddy talking on phone. That daddy talking to other daddy."

They are all David. They all sound like David. They all look like David. They can never be David.

We are at the commissary shopping for our weekly groceries. She is calm. She rides in the cart with her hands full of snacks, and Elijah rides on my hip in his carrier. All is well. We move up and down the aisles while I chatter about snacks and juice and a promised cookie.

"Look those two daddies. I want talk to them," she says.

I look up to find two soldiers moving through the aisle. "They are busy. They are shopping, too." I try to avoid her pleas. We can't get away from them. They are in every aisle. They are behind us, in front of us, and to the side of us.

She starts crying. "I want talk to those daddies." The tears in her eyes break me.

I relent. "Excuse me, sir. Could you please talk to my daughter? Her daddy is in Iraq right now and she is obsessed with all of you in uniform." I talk fast, hoping to keep his attention. "She may call you a daddy, but she knows that you are not her daddy."

He looks extremely uncomfortable. "I don't want her to call me Daddy. I am not her daddy," he replies. I try to avoid the anger rising in my chest. I can't blame him. He doesn't know about the endless nights she spent screaming and pleading for him. He can't know or understand her pain.

"She knows that. Could you just please talk to her. She misses him," I beg.

"Um, okay. Sure." He walks over to her slowly, unsure of what to say. I can tell he has no children of his own. He has no clue what we are going through. I am grateful that he is willing to talk. "Hello," he says as she looks to her feet. "Hi," she mumbles, shying away from him.

He looks to the other soldier for direction. He shrugs his shoulders and continues to try to chat. "What are you doing?" He is uneasy. He bounces from foot to foot.

"Shopping." She is quiet. She stares at his uniform. She reaches out with a scared hand. She is nervous, but it is almost as if there is another force at work inside of her. Her hand touches his uniform. She runs her fingers over his patches. She leans across the cart to touch his nametag. She is dissecting him. She is willing him to be David. She is trying to touch her daddy any way she can.

Watching her is agonizing, and I can hardly contain my emotions. I am empty and full at the same time. Tears ease the pain, but never get rid of it. "My daddy at work." She holds up her head and meets his eyes.

He stops fidgeting, and he touches her little hand. "He will be home soon, I'm sure," he says quietly.

He looks at me uneasily. There is compassion in his eyes, and he holds out his arms, and hugs her. She clings to him. She doesn't want to let go. He holds her until she is willing to part with him.

"Thank you so much." He turns to walk away, and she begins to babble again. The moment is gone, but it feels like an eternity has passed.

Fresh Air

I try never to make eye contact with men. If I look into their eyes, they may see just how lonely I am. They may see how much I miss having David sleep next to me. They may see the vacant place inside me. I cannot allow myself to wander into another man's eyes because I don't want to allow any room between me and David. We are far enough from each other. I can't allow a fissure to break and become a canyon.

When the maintenance man enters my house to install an air conditioner, I refuse to look into his eyes. I let him through the door, and I listen to his explanation about his work. But I busy myself with the kids. I do not talk to him. I do not look at him. I try to pretend he doesn't exist.

His cologne will not allow me. My nose is filled with his smell. I am intoxicated by the smell of oil, dirt, sweat, and deodorant. I finally look at him. He is quiet. He is tall. He is muscular.

"We will need to cut a hole in your wall, ma'am. It may get cold in here." I do not respond. I am no longer listening. His eyes are blue. They are calm. They are fiery. They are strong.

196

I cook breakfast for the kids while I watch him work, and I begin to wander through our indiscretion. The sound of him working begins to trail off in my mind while I imagine what could be between the two of us.

His long, strong fingers wrap around the handle of a shovel. He is whistling while he pushes and pulls the snow. His fingers are tight. They are gripping the wood. He is having his way with the snow.

He drops tools onto the garage floor. He is changing the oil. The oil falls into the pan, and I am intoxicated by the smell. I can only see his legs from under the truck. He uses the wrench to tighten the oil filter. It is music to my ears.

His strong, muscular legs push the lawn mower through the jungle of green behind our house. I smell his sweat and listen as the mower hums and snaps through the weeds. His arms flex, and his chest glistens. I smell the clean grass, the fresh, invigorating smell of mulch. It is an aphrodisiac.

I lie in bed listening to the children waking in the morning. Elijah is crying for me to pick him up. Amelia calls for me to play. The familiar tiredness and dread of a new day move through my aching body. He leans over to me and whispers in my ear, "You stay in bed. I will take the children all day. You don't have to do anything." I lie there and relish the feeling of the covers falling over my head. I curl my legs, stretch my arms, and fall into a deep sleep.

His strong hands lift pots and pans from the cabinet. He is making dinner for me and the kids. His hands move quickly and carnally over the ingredients. He is chopping the vegetables with those strong hands. He is demanding of them. He is forthright with them. He uses those strong hands to set the table, pull out my chair, and place the napkin gently in my lap. I inhale his creation and exhale with satisfaction.

He clears the table and begins to do the dishes. The muscles in his arms flex and retract while scraping the pans. He is forceful with them. He is violent with his demands of them. I sit at the table and listen to the sound of water running over them and the clanking of dishes as they are dried and put back into their places.

I relish the thought of our indiscretion. I could stay there, wandering through it for hours, but his voice snaps me back to reality. "Excuse me, ma'am. Your air conditioner should be fine now. If you have any trouble, please call the housing office and let them know. You have a nice day now." "Thank you," I say, blushing and immediately terrified he has seen the visions behind my eyes. I wonder if he noticed me watching him.

I close the door behind him, and guilt begins to engulf me. I wait nervously for David's call. I need to tell him. If I keep it from him, then I am afraid that I will become open to the possibility of what I imagined.

When he calls, I am near tears. There is no bounce in my voice, and he notices. "You okay?" he asks. "No. There was a man here today working on the air conditioner." He sucks in his breath. I know he is worried about what I am getting ready to tell him.

"I really liked him, David, and I feel horrible because I imagined being with him." "You mean you wanted to sleep with him?" he asks quietly. "No! I didn't even consider that. It wasn't a physical thing at all," I try to explain.

"I don't understand. How did you want to be with him?" he asks nervously. I answer, "I wanted him to stay here with me and take care of me. I wanted him to cut the grass, to change the oil, to shovel the snow, and to do anything to take a little pressure off me." He is quiet. "David?"

"Yeah, I'm here." I can tell he is smiling and laughing at me. "What?" I ask. He responds, "You just miss a man, honey. That's natural. When we go to the Green Zone, and there are civilian women there, we all sit and stare at them because they aren't in uniforms. They are wearing shorts, not short shorts, just shorts. And we can't stop staring because we haven't seen a woman's legs in so long. It is hard not to look."

"So you feel this way, too?" I ask. "Yeah. A year is a long time. I can smell their perfume from twenty yards away. They smell so clean. They smell like flowers," he explains. "They smell like women, and it makes me think of your shower gel. It makes me think of you using my razor to shave your legs. It makes me really miss something feminine."

His answer eases my guilt but not enough to satisfy my mind. "Are you sure you aren't mad at me, David? I actually pictured him being here with me. I imagined him in your place," I say. He laughs and says, "You are so sweet. How could I be mad at you? I put you there in that situation."

"I know, David. But I don't need some guy to change the oil. Dad didn't raise me to depend on any man. I can do it myself. You know that about me. Why would I think of this particular guy like this? Why would I even want him around?"

"Because he was in your house doing my job. And you didn't have to do it yourself. Even if it was for only a few hours," he says quietly. I can tell it bothers him for someone to even momentarily replace him, even if he refuses to admit it. "I know you can change the oil. I know you can do it all. I have seen you. It isn't about that," he says. My feelings for him overwhelm me. There are times when he stops my heart. Sometimes I forget about his ability to do that.

"I love you, David. Do you know that? Do I make you feel that?" I ask him. "Of course you do. You just did."

I smile, blush, and spend the rest of our ten minutes talking about our plans for the day. I hang up the phone, begin to cook dinner, and savor the cool air moving through our house.

Avoiding the Turbulence

Amelia and I are grooving again. We are in sync. We are functioning as our own little unit. We have a routine, and she is thriving in that. She talks to David every morning, and then we fill the void throughout the day: playing outside, going to gymnastics, meeting friends at McDonald's, and visiting friends for play dates.

We do anything to forget and leave behind the silence of our house. Neither one of us enjoys the emptiness of it. We function, but constant moving makes everything bearable.

She knows when she will eat. She knows when she will sleep. She knows she will hear her daddy's voice in the morning. I pray she will hear his voice. I try not to let my mind wander into that fear. I try not to nurture the knowledge of every military family's reality.

But there are moments, frightening moments, when I realize that every person has a limit. In the back of my mind, I know that he can only go over there so many times unharmed before he comes home to us broken, mended, or empty.

Or maybe he will never come home to us. He isn't superhuman. Those moments are too scary for me. They are too real.

I have to walk back into the bubble of never-neverland. It is a false world I have created around me, my children, and my computer husband. We talk about our routine. We have lengthy discussions about what Amelia and Elijah eat for breakfast. We debate at length about what they are going to do in the afternoon. We plan fun things so that we can all forget that we are not together.

David watches Amelia spin and dance on the computer. It is our lifeline. It keeps us connected and in charge of our marriage. He listens to Elijah babbling toward the computer screen. He is having a conversation with his two-dimensional daddy. Amelia has learned to show the web cam her boo-boos. She talks to it when she needs to tell David something. She believes he is watching her sleep when I unplug the web cam and put it in her room.

This is our reality, and we are functioning. We pretend David is sitting in the living room watching us rather than on a computer thousands of miles away. It is a routine of pretending that everything is okay. It is a routine of pretending that we are not all just passing time until he comes home. We are pretending we are all happy and choosing to believe it is all going to be over soon.

We do whatever it takes to get us through the day because that is another day closer to seeing his face or to feeling his breath in my ear. We continue to do whatever it takes to be whole again.

Celebrity Spotting

Sometimes I don't understand what David is a part of or what my kids and I have become a part of. I question the decision to invade Iraq. I question the decision to go to war. I question the decision to leave these men and women in harm's way while their families hope and pray for their safe return. There are no answers anywhere.

It is so hard to know what is right or wrong. I know that a military wife is expected not to ask these questions. But I often wonder how realistic that is, and whether it's right. This war can't continue without questions of its worth. I'm sure David has these questions. Or ones similar in nature. I'm sure he wonders exactly why they are there and what they are doing.

I see the news on occasion. More are killed, wounded, or violated. The body count grows. There is no end in sight. I hate myself when I breathe a sigh of relief upon realizing it is not his unit that has been mortared, shot, wounded, bombed, or mutilated. I hold my breath momentarily until I read the names of the fallen, or I make it through the day without that dreaded knock on the door or the phone call. I feel guilty when I am thankful that it was another man or woman who died or was wounded. They are all someone's brother, sister, mother, father, daughter, son, aunt, uncle, cousin, or friend. They are all someone.

In my heart, I know where I stand, but I have no idea where I *should* stand. The only thing that resonates with me as a military wife is that I know I stand by David. His face is in every soldier's on the news. They all have that mixture of doubt, anger, and fear. I see the proud smiles of countless faces, and the roaming eyes of the soldiers. I wonder if he is there with them.

I often wonder if he is there on the news. Days and weeks of wondering how long it will take before he appears on television are answered in one news story. The reporters are returning to Haifa Street in Iraq. It was the most dangerous street in Iraq at the beginning of the war. They are going back to see the changes and to gauge the success of the war.

The general of the Iraqi army is the centerpiece of the story. He is walking and waving his hands to his people. I look closely for David. This is his mission for the day. There are soldiers behind the general, guarding him, and then, I see David. I see his face and recognize his body. I know it is him. It is just a glimpse of him, but I know that I am witnessing his day.

The reporter talks to the Iraqi people and interviews them about their safety. They appear ecstatic that we are there. I am unsure of what they really feel, of what they want to say or what they truly mean. But, for the moment, because our news says so, I am convinced of the need for us. I see their smiling faces and want to believe that the interpreter is speaking their truthful words.

The soldiers move through the street. They are patrolling and doing their jobs. But they stop, only for a moment, and play with the kids, and I know that David is one of them. My David is a magnet for children.

I imagine his smile and his sparkling eyes behind his goggles. I can only see the soldiers from the nose down. They each carry a rifle in one hand, and their hands are prepared. They are waiting and watching.

It is surreal to see him there on the television. It is amazing to see him walking through the streets of Baghdad. My heart pounds in my chest as I wonder what I could possibly witness. I wonder what I could see happen to him right in front of me. I look to the mosques in the background, and I pray that no one will implode on the screen. The Iraqi general walks through the streets, and I beg David not to get too close to him. I am afraid he is an important and obvious target.

It is hard to see them worried. It is painful to see them on edge and in danger. It is hard to accept that he provides for us by putting himself on the line every day, every hour. I try once again to imagine what he must be feeling about it all. To figure out exactly what I feel about it. It is a jumbled mess. I worry for him. I worry that he may be losing himself in a sea of doubt and anger or that he may be exhausted from giving everything he has. I worry that he will never be the same man again. That he will never be able to smile again. I know he has seen and been through so much.

But, there on the screen, they smile at the children. They play with them on the street. His load seems lighter, and he is still so alive and so vibrant. He still can see the good in the small faces that run to him. I know he hasn't lost himself. He hasn't let this war take from him what he holds dearest.

He is smiling at these kids. He is laughing. I know that he is thinking of his children, and I know he is missing them. He is happy to play with them, but he is holding his biggest smile just for us. He is keeping that part of his heart safe and locked away. That much I do know.

It is only for a minute that I see him, and it is only a glimpse into his everyday life. I know it is skewed by the media and that this is not indicative of how he feels on a daily basis. But I am thankful to see it. I am thankful to have that image in my head. I am thankful to know that he is still striving to work it all out. He is still looking to the future. He is still willing and able to laugh no matter the circumstances.

And today is one day when he won't have to try to explain to me what he did.

Below the Belt

David sends pictures of his surroundings nearly every day. I scroll through pictures of him working, of what he is seeing, what he has seen, and who or what is seeing him. There are pictures of beautiful architecture, mosques, palm trees, and sand. There are also pictures of sandstorms, improvised explosive devices, bombed trucks and buildings, burned mosques, weapons caches, and people with fear in their eyes. He sends pictures of people filled with hatred.

I want to believe he is on some kind of vacation. Or that he is sending me pictures from summer camp.

I look at the pictures of women hiding their faces, of men watching David closely while he takes the picture, of wreckage from previous bombings, and I try to believe he is safe. I try to believe nothing is going to happen to him. He sends me packages of postcards, Iraqi army patches, our children's portraits painted by Iraqi hands, and CDs full of pictures.

I look at each CD with a feeling of dread and expectation. I want to know what he is doing, to see what he is seeing and who is seeing him. I want to know what his life is like there. I want to be a part of what he is witnessing, what he is going through. I want to see it.

He sends me videos. I wait patiently for them to load. There on a grainy computer screen is my husband riding in his truck through Baghdad, through the wires, through the palm trees, past the mosques, and around the eyes that are searching for him. It is a scene that I could only imagine in an action movie.

From the right of the screen there is a line of fire, almost like fireworks being thrown through the air. Then there is chaos. The grainy computer screen becomes black. Then brown with mud. Then grainy again. David throws a man to the ground. His boot is near the man's head. His gloved hand holds the gun to the man's head. I recognize his hand. The same hand that holds my face and my children's tiny fingers.

In a flash, there is his face again. David's beautiful face covered in gear, wearing goggles, and a helmet. He clutches his gun, and he wears a bulletproof vest. David hands his gun to someone. He pushes the man who continues to try to get up. He searches him, holds him, searches him again, and pushes him to the ground again. The view moves from the ground to the sky.

They are moving again. The screen is grainy, full of mud, and the truck is moving again. The screen goes black.

My heart pounds. My body is cold. My stomach convulses. My entire nervous system is being mutilated. I stare at the screen, and I realize I have the power to watch it again and again and again.

I click on the green arrow, and watch my husband being attacked. Over and over and over again. Each time, I am not sure how to label my emotion. I become unsure of my ability to breathe. Unsure of my ability to believe what is on the screen. I can process nothing, and I am sure that I will never be able to get up from this computer again.

I watch David's finger. Watch it twitch just for a moment on the trigger. I stop the video to see if I can distinguish whether he hesitated, whether he considered killing the man. I watch his foot. I wonder if he wants to kick him. I wonder if he wants to beat him.

I wonder if he wants to watch him bleed in the street, if he wants to watch him die there next to the palm trees, next to the sand and the mosques.

I watch every second, frame by frame, until my body contorts with anger. I want this man dead. Obliterated. I am so full of rage. He tried to kill my husband. In front of my eyes, while I watched on a computer screen, he tried to kill my husband. I want David to shoot him. I want him to kick him. To mutilate him. I want him to feel every ounce of pain that he could have inflicted on my family. I want him to pay for nearly widowing me. I want him to pay for nearly taking a devoted father from his innocent children.

I watch it over and over again, each time becoming more enraged until I finally stop on that one moment when David looks straight into the camera. The look on his face freezes me. I can see his hazel eyes. His lips. His nose and his wrinkled forehead. I can see his fear, his anger, his adrenaline, his determination, his pride, and his desire to see his children again.

I can see his turmoil and his realization of what is important to him. I can see it all in those eyes. They are like fire coming out from the screen to meet me. I focus on his eyes and lock the video on his stare. It all passes into me, pours into me, out of him, and into my veins. My body aches. My mind races. I have no idea how to stop the twitching and convulsing inside me. His eyes are piercing and wild. The pain of his daily struggles and the determination to fight for his life, to destroy whomever it is that would see him dead, fuel him. My anger explodes, and I welcome the boiling rage in his steely stare. I want them dead, too.

Hours later, I finally turn off the video, but his eyes stay with me. This is the closest I will ever get to experiencing what he is going through on a daily basis. I was there with him. There is a change in me, a shift. We will never be the same again. We will never be able to go back.

We did not choose the battle. But within us is a basic need to survive and to see each other again. I have now seen his determination to make this happen. He didn't choose the war. He chose a job. Today, I thank God that he did his job.

Vacancy

Before David left for Iraq, he quietly and calmly placed a green journal on our bookshelf. He never mentioned it, and I never felt the need to question him. I knew what was in it. I just never wanted to face the reality of what it contained.

After watching his attack, I know I need to read it. I need to face it all: the fears and reality of this deployment. I walk to the bookshelf and pull the journal from its perch. Inside, in David's handwriting, are the words, "If I should die."

I check on the kids once more before attempting to read his letters to his family. I make sure they are content and sleeping. Then walk to the couch, put a blanket over my legs, and begin to read.

His first letter is to me. "To my beautiful wife." I read his wishes and promises. He writes of his love, his trust, and his devotion. He tells me of his desire for me to continue with life, to fight for love, and to push myself to always be the mother and woman that he loves. His vivid memories of my wedding dress and of the first time he saw me smile weave through his written promises of a limitless love that will endure long after his passing.

My body is racked with sobs, and my eyes burn. I push myself to read his letter to Amelia. "To my precious princess." I hold my stomach in while I read about the first moments he saw her. The first moments he touched her. Even his written words to her are tender and protective. He speaks about his desire for true love and devotion for her. I scan his list of what future boyfriends should know about his little girl. I read his plan for her life and his dream for her happiness.

I want to stop, to never face this pain, but I make myself read his declaration to Elijah. "To my handsome son." He speaks of his pride in Elijah. He tells him to always respect women and to love his mother and wife with all of his heart. He tells him to push himself, but to never be afraid to cry. He tells him to always live with pride, honor, and self-respect.

I make myself read every word. He deserves that much out of me.

For too long, I have been weak. I have been on a roller coaster of emotions pretending to know and understand what this deployment really means. I have accepted the praise from strangers. Then pushed aside the politics of it. I have ignored the happenings, avoided all that is real and violent and honest and pushed it to the back of my mind. I have been floating through this deployment, wishing for a way to ignore it, deny it, or pretend it doesn't exist. While he fights, avoids bombs, and dodges death.

I begged David to show me what he was going through on a daily basis. I asked him to help me understand. When he wrote letters of being attacked or told me what he has witnessed, I crumbled and failed him. I cried, and he stood strong, comforting me in my weakness.

The video of his attack has devastated me. It has broken me. It has drenched me with reality and has crushed the bubble that I had built to nurse me through this deployment.

I read his words to us now, and force myself to accept the bitter truth of this situation. There is no more pretending for me. I no longer have the ability to assume that the one fighting on the news is another man, husband, or father. There is no more imagining David on the news. There is no more wondering if he is fighting. There is no wanting to see his face during the attacks. There is no more doubt of his worry, of his composure. All these questions and deceptions have been answered in one short video.

He is the news.

He is being bombed. Being shot at. Being hated. He could be kidnapped. Tortured. Beheaded. Burned. Mutilated. For months on end, he has been facing and accepting the reality that he may never see us again. He has been pushing through each day with strength, determination, and dignity. He accepted the truth of this deployment long before he ever left us. It is my turn to face that reality. It is my turn to accept this life.

I am changed. I am somber. I am a potential widow. With friends, I no longer wish to talk about celebrities and their adopted children. At home, I have no desire to watch television shows about housewives being desperate or about singing idols.

Anything and anyone not involved in this deployment has wandered out of my realm of understanding. I know I need to stay connected, to attempt to be involved with people that do not live on Army bases. I want to remember how to have polite, casual conversations. Not everyone can be conscious of this deployment all the time. I try to comprehend the outside world, to read magazines or engage in social discussions. I can't connect.

I have finally learned to function like a robot. I am efficient and productive, but I have no empathy. My emotions will not interfere with what I have to do. I have no compassion and no sympathy. I have no sadness. No anger. No depression. I have nothing. I am vacant.

I smile for my children, laugh for them, play with them. But I only truly connect with someone when I am talking on the computer with David. His eyes reflect our reality. I understand his inability to laugh. I respect his silence. I relate to his emotionless letters. I welcome his empty stares and half attempts at conversation.

Nothing will ever be the same again, no matter how much we wish for it to be.

I understand why he can feel nothing. I now feel nothing. Watching his video changed everything. I am not angry with him for sending it to me. I am thankful. I asked him to let me into his life. He did, and now we are finally fighting this war together. We are united in our understandings and our ability to disconnect from anything outside of our reality.

I take the CD of his attack and tape it to the inside of his journal. I close it softly and return it to the bookshelf. I respect each of them for what they have shown me, and I pray that I will never see either of them again.

Sharp Edges

Will I be the wife David remembers, the wife he wants? Will I be too cold for him? Too rough, too independent, or too self-sufficient? I am trying to remember myself before this deployment, before this war, before this enlistment. I am trying to remember the smile that he loves, searching for the touch that he craves. Anything that will welcome him home.

Before this deployment, I was full of egotistical beliefs that our relationship could withstand anything. I foolishly believed nothing could touch us. Nothing could burn, tinge, or demolish the life we built together. We faced the painful uncertainty of reunion after his deployment to Afghanistan. We loved each other enough to reintroduce ourselves. We have learned to weather separation. We have learned to deny temptation. No person or situation could divide us. Except death. I was naïve to dismiss the possibility that he could die. Stupidly, I believed that not even death could touch us. The realization that I may never see him again grips me. I need to see him again just to tell him I know what it means to live with him now.

I knew nothing of life before this deployment. Nothing of pain and nothing of loss. I knew nothing of missing someone or the strength of a union. This deployment slapped me in the face with reality. With love. With strength. With undying devotion and with a newfound belief in my wedding vows.

I miss that naïve girl, but I am stronger than she was. And colder. I can never again be the girl he once knew.

David has had a similar revelation. It is embedded in the long pauses in our conversations. Our love is thicker, but the expectation of our reunion is heavy. He is carrying the weight of uncertainty with me. He is feeling the same way. I can see the fear in his eyes when he talks to me on the computer. I can see the harshness in his face. It all hides beneath the lines that caress his face. He is older, deadened, emptier, and stronger.

I feel it. I see it. He has to be feeling the same aura from me. We have the same monotonous voice. We have similar actions and feelings. All rough and sharp.

I search myself for softness, some remnant of a woman. I hope for some delicate feature to share with him. I buy new clothes, new perfumes, and new makeup. I paint my nails and my toenails and treat myself to long baths in hopes of softening my edges. Maybe my soft exterior will lessen the blow of the concrete inside.

Standing Still

Summer has hit us with a vengeance. Today is the Fourth of July, and it is stifling. I sit outside and sip orange juice. The kids are still asleep. The birds in the trees call for the day to begin. It is six in the morning, and my pajamas are stuck to my skin.

The computer buzzes me from the living room, announcing David's request to talk. He is not as busy now that his missions are all but over, and he sits in Baghdad waiting for his ride home. He is more than ready to leave the sand, and he usually wakes me every morning, eager to feel like a vibrant part of his family again. This morning he is impatient and rings the messenger doorbell several times.

His voice softly flows through the speaker, but it isn't quiet enough. "I want talk to Daddy, too!" Amelia screams from her bed. She knows the buzzing from the computer speakers means that David is online. I go to her room and open the door. David waits.

"Daddy want talk to me?" I pick her up and walk through the house. "Of course he does. Who wouldn't want to talk to you?" I am thankful for these moments with him. I know I need to be thankful that we get to see him every morning now. But I hate that she has adapted to this lifestyle. She and Elijah have to settle for his face and not his body.

We have a new microphone on the computer. It frees me to move away from the screen. I am no longer a prisoner of the headphones. I fix breakfast in the kitchen while Amelia and David talk. I can hear their conversation, and I can answer his questions from the kitchen. He knows I cannot stop my day for him, and he accepts my faceless voice.

Elijah is awake. His growing cry blasts from the monitor. I lift him from his crib. "Daddy wants to see you, little man." I put him in his saucer, fix his cup of milk, and listen as David talks and sings to him. "Does he drink just milk now?" David's voice asks. "Yeah. He completely refused to nurse any longer. Breaks my heart," I explain.

I move through the house, making beds and getting clean clothes for the day. "What are your plans for today?" he calls from the living room. "Not much. Nothing is going on here today. They had Mountainfest last week, so there will be no fireworks or anything like that." There is nothing going on anywhere on base. The Tenth Mountain Division has three brigades. David is in First Brigade. Second Brigade will be leaving for Iraq in a couple of weeks. Third Brigade is in Afghanistan. The base is empty. I'm not sure there are any spare hands to light fireworks.

I fumble through the kids' drawers and decide to muster some Independence Day spirit, pulling out their new red, white, and blue clothes. Amelia has a new "tutu" that has been taunting her in her closet. I get it for her and pause for a moment, looking at and touching the size on the tag. The numbers have changed five times since David left. Elijah's have changed four times. Time has moved on without David.

We move through the morning with little motivation to do anything. It is too hot. I pull a chair into the shade and start the sprinkler for the kids. Amelia runs through it in her tutu and squeals when the cold water catches her. Elijah sits just out of the water's reach. He puts his hand in the stream long enough to feel a bit of relief.

It's quiet outside. No grills are scenting the air. Hardly any children are out playing. There are no bikes, no bouncing basketballs. It isn't the Fourth of July that I once imagined and experienced on a base. No bands playing. No parades.

I sit in the stillness of the day and stare down my street. There are rows of flags flying. They are all well preserved. My own flag snaps in the wind, and I wonder what David is doing right now. Does he even know what day it is?

It is hard to celebrate, knowing that they will be home soon. It feels premature. I am afraid if I light fireworks, have a cookout, go swimming, or just relish this holiday, then I will jinx their return in some way. The eerie absence of the uniform on base is a clear reminder of the turmoil in Afghanistan and Iraq.

I lie awake at night and listen to the fireworks in the distance. The familiar hiss, boom, and the dull roar of the audience. I am happy people are celebrating. I am glad to know life is still moving and thriving. When David comes home safely and is out of harm's way, then we will be able to celebrate our independence.

Impending Arrival

I want David to come home, but I'm not sure how I'm going to give up my independence and allow him to return to his role as father and husband. I don't know if I have the ability to make him feel needed again.

Every job is mine now. I take care of the truck. I take care of cutting the grass. I take out the trash, care for the kids, pay the bills, care for the cats. I take care of the doctor appointments, our loans. I take care of the food, the laundry, the cleaning, the runny noses, the diaper changing, the singing, the rocking, and the cuddling. I do it all by myself. I don't need help. Everything is where it is supposed to be. Everything has a place. Everything has a purpose. Everything but him.

We are a well-oiled, functioning machine, and I am afraid he will come home and be the wrench in our system. Will we recognize one another? What if I haven't done a good enough job of making sure the children know him? What if Amelia is afraid of him or mad at him again, as she was during his two weeks home? What if I cannot hide my fury or harshness from him?

What if I am not the wife he left all those months ago, standing in the parking lot, sobbing? What if I talk differently, walk differently, act differently, cry differently, or don't cry at all? I wonder if he feels the tension. Does he notice that I cannot be fully excited about him coming home? I hope it isn't in my voice. I pray it isn't in my face on the computer or in my letters.

When he came home for two weeks, we knew he would leave again. And we were on our best behavior. I understood that he would need help adjusting, but that it would only be a short time, and then I could release myself of that pressure. Now, he will be home for much longer, and there will be no tiptoeing around our issues. There will be no way to avoid the hovering discussions or the buried pain that will eventually unearth itself. We are no strangers to parting and coming together again, but the fears that burst within me are wispy memories of the pain of readjustment we felt after Afghanistan. We were more open and honest during this deployment. Still, it is all there, bubbling under the surface. And this time he will not be stopping by for a visit. His arrival will be the fuse, igniting a bomb that will undoubtedly explode.

I hope all this doubt and confusion leaves me in the instant I see his face. I hope it flees my body the moment I touch him again. I hope it melts away when he holds me close to him. But I know myself better than that.

Removing My Blinders

Amelia is desperate for attention. I try to give her everything I have, but she only wants her daddy to come home. We take a cake to my friend's husband, who has returned. Amelia tries to figure out why he is here and David isn't. She stares at him, following his every move.

He looks worn, thin, and very happy to be home. I thought Amelia might be angry. Or jealous. But she is hungry. Ravenous. She wants him all to herself. She inches into his presence. She casually pushes his girls aside so she alone can smell him, touch him, and feel him. She will stop at nothing to feel like David is here.

I'm so grateful he welcomes her, taking her onto his lap to share his cake. She becomes the only child in the room. He holds her tightly and talks to her about David. He tells her that her father will be home soon, too, and that he loves her. She's shaking, overwhelmed, but happy. She says nothing.

As he gets up to walk across the room, she follows him, touching the back of his leg.

I can hardly contain myself when I see her beautiful, tiny hand reach up to touch him. She is hungry with the need to be held and to be in strong arms. She follows him through the house, her hand never leaving his leg. He lets her. He helps her and encourages her. He walks slowly to make sure she can keep up.

I try to hide my fear and rising tears from her. I walk into my friend's kitchen, out of Amelia's sight, and cry. Around the corner, Amelia is again sitting on his lap. She touches his face and holds his hand. I want to touch David, but I can understand and voice that. She only has her overwhelming need and inability to identify her confusion to guide her small hands. Her desire to feel David and her raw hurt overshadow anything I could ever want.

I am afraid to look at her, to watch her beam at his face. I am terrified to see her smile at him. We only have a few weeks left before David comes home. I cannot break until he is here. I cannot allow myself to melt. Nor can I bring myself to take her away from this scene.

My friend stands next to me. She says nothing. She doesn't touch me or hold me. She doesn't need to. She meets my teary eyes with tears of her own. It's a pain she has experienced intimately. "I can't bear this," I tell her. She looks deeply into my eyes. She holds them. Her brown eyes mirror mine. I look to the ceiling, inhaling a long, deep breath before I look into her eyes again. I nod and brush away the tears. We stand side by side, and we both look to Amelia.

I don't want to tell her that we need to go. I don't want to take this from her. But he has his own family to love, touch, and caress. They are waiting patiently for us to leave so that they can reclaim him.

When he tells her goodbye, he holds her lovingly and respectfully. He sees his daughters in her, and it's more than I could ask for from him.

Our house seems all the more empty after seeing our friends' fullness. But Amelia skips in. She is happy. She has been held by strong arms that look like David's. She is close to David now, and I pray that this moment lasts until he touches her again.

No Promises Made

David may be home in a few weeks. Earlier than we expected. If it happens. There are always extensions. There is a possibility that he may be over there for three more months. His brigade will return in sections from the middle of July through early August, and I have no idea when he will board his plane. He joined up with his already deployed unit after Elijah's birth, so his late arrival could mean he is one of the last ones home. Each passing hour pushes on me the anticipation and dread of him coming home. I am not sure when I will see him or when I will hear from him. I try to keep my mind clear, to not think of when he will be here, or if he will be here, but I continue to muddle my brain with one continuous thought.

How will he come home to me?

I walk through the commissary, and I see amputees there buying groceries, continuing to function despite their missing legs, their missing arms, their missing hands, fingers, feet, and toes. Their faces are tired, worn, uncertain, and reserved. I wonder, are they still married, still getting married, planning to be married, still

221

in a relationship? Do they remember the moment they lost the limb? Can they still feel it, and do they still try to scratch an itch that is no longer there?

I want to ask how they were attacked. Were they warned, were they surprised, or did they expect to lose more? I cannot imagine their recovery. Do they question why they lost a piece of themselves? How many pieces of them are lost? Are they are bitter? Have they written congressmen and senators demanding answers for their missing arms, hands, legs, feet, fingers, and toes?

I wonder if they are satisfied with the answers. Were they proud to serve? Are they fine with the remains of their bodies, and only half mourn the loss of the other pieces? I wonder if their wives or husbands are accepting and barely notice the change. If their girl-friends or friends fail to see a difference in their demeanor.

How will he come home to me?

I take Amelia and Elijah to the doctor for checkups. I am concerned about their shots, worried for their pain.

The man sitting next to me has been badly burned. He has no nose. His eyes are tight. He has little hair left. His taut skin ripples in waves of tan and red. I wonder if his wife, girlfriend, or friends have learned not to notice the difference. I wonder how he was attacked. How he lost the skin on his body. I want to ask if they had to cut off his uniform. I want to know how long he sat in recovery waiting for his bandages to be wrapped and rewrapped, and for his skin to be pulled and treated to create new elasticity. I want to know if he still hurts, if he still feels like his skin is on fire. I want to know how many surgeries he has had in attempts to grow, create, and implant new life into his old skin.

Amelia stares at him. "Say 'Hi,' Amelia," I urge. She curls into my legs. She has seen burn victims before, but that doesn't mean she's used to it.

"Hi," she says as she digs her fingers into my thighs.

"I have one her age at home," he says through skin that used to be his mouth.

"They are a handful aren't they?" I ask. Not sure if he has a hand left to fill.

"They sure are. My son is all over the place running and playing all the time." He continues to watch and wave at Amelia. She stares in return.

I wonder if other people choose to look him in the eyes and see him for the father that he still is. I want to ask him if he is okay with the stares that come his way. What is it that allows him to still see the beauty in the smile of a little girl? Would he go back there again and fight the same war?

Our name is called and we stand to walk into the office. "Bye," Amelia says to him unprompted.

"Bye, sweetie," he calls to her. I look back at him and smile one last time. He looks at me, but I cannot tell if he is smiling. His charred skin will not allow him that luxury.

How will he come home to me?

We walk through the clinic after the shots, and walk by the counseling room. Today there is an AA meeting.

Too many men and women come home and drink endlessly. They drink to ease the transition. They drink to dull the explosions. They drink to forget. Some of them become angry when they drink. They lose the inhibitions that hold them in a vise grip. They unleash the burden that they carry only when they can no longer walk the white line. Others are sad, but numbed by drinking. Still others become loud and belligerent, daring anyone to question their choices.

Alcohol isn't the only drug of choice for the veterans. They snort cocaine off the hoods of cars, or they inject drugs directly into the bloodstream to dull the screams, to erase the memories. Anything to slow their racing minds, to escape.

How will he come home to me?

I drive home from the doctor and see the new "presents" that have been given to and bought by soldiers coming home. They are fast. They are bright and shiny. There are new trucks, cars, SUVs, motorcycles, and boats everywhere. I drive by them, and see the men and women who drive crazily, angrily, and devastatingly fast. I listen to the stories of men being pried out of cars, pulled away from guardrails, and scraped off the pavement. They lie helpless in a hospital while tubes feed them. They stand quietly during the funerals of those who died in the car next to them while they drove haphazardly through their pain. They are trying to leave it behind them. They can never go fast enough to drown it out.

How will he come home to me?

Friends talk about their husbands asking for a divorce and about their desire for one. They have changed. They have moved on. They cannot manage a marriage thousands of miles apart. They have been cheating. David talks of his friends who are getting divorced. They are tired of their wives draining their bank accounts while they are deployed. They are intolerant of their wives' new boyfriends, or old boyfriends, or secret girlfriends. They are tired of being tired of each other. They talk of the pain of separation or disappointment and broken hearts of those who did not wait at home.

They speak of painful reunions, of angry children, and of the inability to be patient. They mention the reality of a changed heart, a deadened one, and an empty one. There is no way to avoid the return of a different, depressed, timid, or explosive soldier. There is no way to ease the transitioning heart.

How will he come home to me?

I read books about post-traumatic stress disorder. Talk to friends who have been through this several times before. I've been through it, too, but this time is different. This war is different. They speak of anger. They whisper of denial. They worry about emotional outbursts and uncontrollable crying. They warn me of quiet submersion. They warn me of isolation and silence. They warn me of night terrors, of sweaty pillows, and of waking with his hands around their necks. They talk about the fear for their children and their torment for their husband. They speak of their inability to understand or to relate to him. They speak of their anger that they cannot understand him or tolerate him any more.

How will he come home to me?

I drive past the memorial statue on base. The flag flies at half-mast. Men in uniform carry a coffin. It is draped in a flag. There are chairs under the tent, and people huddle around the wife of a hero. I stop as the men begin the slow folding of the flag. They are meticulous. They are sure of each move and of each turn. They have done this before. They hold it delicately and place it into her hands. She falls over the flag and looks to the sky for reprieve. She has two children next to her. They salute his coffin, and a bugle begins those slow, painful notes in the distance.

I want to hold her. To envelope her. I want to end the pain for her, to end it for all of us. I want him to get out of the coffin, put his arms around her, and walk her down the aisle again.

How will he come home to me?

At Last

5:30 a.m. July 19, 2006.

David's portion of his brigade is coming home today. He is flying overhead somewhere in a huge Army plane, stuffed like a sardine, with hundreds of other soldiers leaving Iraq. I imagine him sitting in his metal chair against the wall of the plane, his helmet on, his armor strapped to his chest, holding his gun for the duration of the flight. They are ready. Always ready to fight and defend. I imagine the smile bursting from his face, from all their faces, as they wait for their first glimpse of home.

He is supposed to be here at 3:00 in the afternoon, but Amelia and Elijah don't know. I can't tell Amelia. Not yet. She will go insane with excitement. I can't tell her until we are on our way to get him. There can always be delays, extensions, or security breaches. To think of him being delayed is agonizing for me. I would rather shelter her from the possibility of that pain. I can't watch tears of anger, sorrow, and disappointment spill on her face. Not again.

8:00: I cook Amelia and Elijah breakfast, trying not to imagine and linger on the breakfast we may have tomorrow. The one that has clouded my dreams: cream cheese, cereal, and Amelia and Elijah laughing next to their daddy.

I push through the morning, trying to ignore the fluttering in my stomach and the impatient thoughts swirling in my mind. It is agony waiting for the day to unfold, and I try to keep our routine going just to alleviate the excitement that could overtake me.

"Daddy on the computer this morning?" Amelia asks.

"No, honey. Daddy can't get on this morning," I explain, trying to contain myself. Her drooping shoulders urge more of an answer. "He is busy, but I'm sure you will see him soon." She wants to cry, but my bursting smile keeps her tears from falling. She begins to play with her toys, and I silently plead with her to ask no more questions.

12:00: I stand at the window every five minutes, hoping to hear the sound of his plane landing on the base airfield close to our house. I feel foolish, giddy. I am tingling, shaking, stuttering, and completely petrified.

I pace the floor. Check my hair again. Reapply makeup. I call my mother, call my friends, call my father, call my brother, and call my friends again. I call anyone who wants to hear my excitement. I talk to anyone who wants to feel it. I call over and over again trying to eat away the three hours I have left. I am overflowing.

Three hours until he is home again. At least on base. We will have to wait hours before he is in our living room, sitting on our couch, holding our children. He will land in three hours, unload equipment from trucks, go to a welcome ceremony, and then he will be all ours.

But, in my mind, three hours are all that separate us. There is no more war. There is no more pain and no more Internet dates. There will be no more delayed phone calls, no more lonely holidays, no more empty nights, no more voiceless stares, no more crying, no more agony, and no more misery. In three hours, I will touch him again.

12:15: I put Amelia and Elijah down for naps. They are fully dressed, and I don't tell Amelia why she is wearing her new special tutu. She asks no questions. It will be a short nap, and they are napping earlier than usual, but I want them to be somewhat rested for him and for the ceremony to come. But Amelia can feel the tension in me. She is excited and hard to calm. It is impossible to calm myself.

I sing to her and tell her stories until she settles in her bed. She finally falls asleep, and I rush through the house to make sure it is clean. I double-check to make sure that I have all the ingredients for his first dinner home. I want no distractions when he gets here. I need him to feel welcome. I want him to feel like he is home. I want it to all be perfect for him. For us.

12:45: I stare at myself again, wishing I had gotten just one more haircut, lost one more pound, and bought one more new outfit. I dissect all that he will see, try to hide the bags under my eyes, and mask the red scratchy veins that have planted themselves in the whites of my eyes. With no way to avoid the souvenirs of this deployment, I turn out the light and concentrate on his loving words and the compliments I know he will shower on me when he finally sees me again.

1:30: I walk through the house, stare out the window, check on the sleeping kids, and stare out the window again. I tidy, dust again, and wander around, looking for something to keep my fidgety hands busy. I try to read to calm my nerves, but the words blur together, and they have no meaning. Nothing but his voice in my ear, his arms around my waist, and his lips on my lips could quiet my racing thoughts and heart.

2:00: In thirty minutes I can leave. I want to be there at least half an hour before his bus rolls in. I only have two miles to drive. Amelia is awake and ready, Elijah is clean and fed, and I pace the floor.

We are supposed to wait until his official welcome-home ceremony before we can see him, but I plan to sneak over to catch him just off the bus or the plane. They can scold me or escort me away. It will be worth it just to see him.

2:10: I can't contain myself in the house any longer. We go to a neighbor's house. I try to talk with my friend, but I can't sit still. Amelia plays with her friends, oblivious to me. Elijah stands next to the couch. He is unsure of himself. He wants to take a step.

"You better not take that step before Daddy sees you," I say jokingly. Elijah isn't walking, isn't talking, and has no teeth. All these milestones that hover around the year mark for most babies have been saved. I know in my heart God has spared David missing these things. He knew David couldn't handle it if he did.

2:20: I can wait no longer. "Amelia, are you ready to go?" I ask, interrupting her play. She's surprised; we've only been here a few minutes.

"No. I playing," she answers.

"Time to go, Amelia. Put away the toys." She starts to whimper.

I meet her whimper with an enormous smile. "Amelia, you have to put away the toys. We are going to get Daddy!" It takes a moment to sink in, to travel to her brain. I see it click. She begins to understand.

She puts away toys with vigor that I have never seen of her. She nearly throws them into their places and runs to get her shoes. She puts them on the wrong feet, grabs her jacket, and yells to me from the door, "Come on, Mommy!"

The two miles between our house and David's company feel like an eternity. I am shaking so hard it's all I can do to drive safely. Amelia is in the backseat chattering away about her daddy. I can't hear her. I can't respond to her. Nothing exists but the road to our reunion.

2:30: I pull into his company parking lot. The plane has already arrived and soldiers, clad in desert uniforms, unload their trucks in a parking lot down the street. Minutes separate us, but there is a soldier standing guard and his anger with me is unmistakable. "You are not supposed to be here ma'am. There is an official welcome-home ceremony in two hours," he growls. "You can pick up your husband then."

I try to look and sound pitiful. "But I was told I may be able to see him here first." Hoping for mercy. "I have a two-year-old back here who is dying to see her daddy," I plead. I don't tell him that the twenty-nine-year-old is the one who cannot be contained. I motion to the rearview mirror. He pokes his head into the truck. Amelia cranes her neck to see him. She looks at his uniform. She is trying to see someone who remotely looks like David.

Another soldier runs to my truck and tells me to pull around to where they are unloading the trucks. "Thank you!" I scream at him. As I pull away, I see the two soldiers arguing with each other in the rearview mirror.

2:35: I pull into the parking lot full of Army uniforms. There is a man holding his baby. His wife is crying. He is crying. I selfishly interrupt them to ask where David is.

He looks at me with sheer joy and tells me to run around the truck to find him. He is only a few feet from me. I leave the kids in their seats. I want to be the first one to see him. I want to be the first one to hold him. I can't share that moment with anyone. Not even our kids. The ten feet that separate us feel like miles.

2:36: I run awkwardly in my black heels and stop at the front of the Army truck. There are hundreds of soldiers unloading equipment. I see him from behind and know instantly it is David. There is a dull ringing in my ears. It is almost impossible to convince myself that he is here, that he is standing in front of me. He is breathing the same air I am, just feet from me.

I stand there, paralyzed. I want to hold this moment. To touch it for years. I want to pull it out of my pocket and talk to it. I want it to become a part of my soul, a part of my past and future. I want to take it into my confidence and make it mine.

He turns toward me, and the shock of seeing me jars him. The green in his eyes begins to sparkle. I run to him. My heels click and snap on the pavement. He runs to me in his desert boots.

As he lifts me into the air, I want to weep in his strong arms, but I can't. I can't cry. I can't laugh. I can't feel anything. Nothing but his arms. I am numb. Something is terribly wrong with me, but I hide my face in his shoulder to avoid showing it.

I take him to the truck where Amelia and Elijah are waiting for him. She is laughing in the window. She is ready for this. She has waited too long. I open the door, and she leans out of her car seat. Her legs swing back and forth, and I have to fight her flailing arms to unbuckle her. I finally get her out of the truck, and she runs to David, then steps away before running to him again. And again.

"Mommy, I want to run Daddy again," she says over and over again. He catches her each time with the same exuberant joy. They both laugh as he lifts her in the air and spins with her. Finally, she is in his strong arms again.

When she allows him, he goes around to the other side of the truck. Timidly, he opens the door. He is unsure of what Elijah will offer. He pulls Elijah out of his car seat.

Elijah smiles his toothless grin, and he pushes his head into David's shoulder. David pulls him to his chest, inhales deeply, and closes his eyes. He rocks Elijah back and forth, and then lifts him high into the air. "I can't believe he isn't scared of me," he says.

"I can," I say.

3:00: With Amelia at his leg, Elijah in his arms, and me by his side, we walk to his company not even thinking of the road that is ahead or the one behind. For now, it is just the four of us. We sit inside the same building where I first left him. I still don't know the name of it. Amelia is on his lap eating popcorn, and Elijah stands between my legs. He teeters back and forth for a moment, and then his hands leave my knees. He picks up his tiny shoe and drops it clumsily in front of him. He moves from a sure step to a stumbling explosion into David's arms.

"Dada," he says as he falls into David's open hands. I meet David's eyes. His tears flow freely. "Was that his first step?" he asks. "That was his first step and his first word," I say.

David pulls him onto his lap alongside his sister. He hugs them both tightly and then he talks softly into Elijah's ear. "Thank you, little man. Thank you for waiting on me."

Recovery

"Womb? Weary?

He rests. He has travelled."

—James Joyce, *Ulysses*

Homecoming

It feels unfamiliar and foreign to have David sitting in the truck next to me. It feels wrong, awkward. Amelia is unsure of herself. She peeks into the seat in front of her, the one that he is in, and says, "Daddy?" "Yeah, baby?" he replies.

"Daddy, you home?" she asks.

David wipes tears from his eyes and clears his throat. "Yeah. I'm home."

"You not going back to work?" she asks.

David bites his bottom lip and replies, "No, baby. I'm not going back to work. Not for a long time." He cuts his words short. He stares out the window and takes a deep breath. "Daddy?"

"Yeah, baby?" he responds. He is answered with silence. She is checking.

"Daddy?" she says again.

"Yeah, baby?" he says, turning around in his seat to look at her.

She says nothing. She only smiles. She is making sure that he hasn't left her.

We pull into the crowded parking lot and David jumps from the truck. He has to find his unit to be part of the official welcome-home ceremony. We struggle to part from him. I don't want him to leave us. He doesn't want to walk away from us.

Amelia cries when he walks away. He closes the truck door, and she begins to whimper. Before I can stop her, she is wailing.

"Honey, Daddy isn't leaving. We are going to meet him inside," I try to soothe her. She doesn't believe me. She screams for him and holds her arms up to the window.

I strap Elijah into the hip carrier, and get her out of the truck. She pushes and pulls against me. "No! Want Daddy!" she screams. We are running late, so I pull her flailing body onto my other hip, and I run across the parking lot.

The band is already playing when we reach the doors. There is nowhere to sit inside the gym. There are hundreds of people there. Children with signs, balloons, and flowers. Husbands and wives on the edges of their seats, waiting to see those faces, that walk, and that uniform coming into the gym. The news is here, too.

The soldiers line up at the entrance, and my breath leaves me. My legs begin to tremble and my heart pounds. I have tears in my eyes. They feel foreign and invasive. I am so emotional, and I am not sure why. This moment is too big for me to understand. It is more than I am. It is more than my kids.

This room contains every tear, every fear, every prayer, every wish, every stolen moment, every lonely night, and every lost morning. Here, in this gym, hovers every empty bed, every dented pillow, every lingering smell of cologne, every piece of rage, regret, anger, frustration, joy, and bittersweet moment. The air is thick with it.

Every person in the gym falls silent just before they enter. Every breath is caught and tears begin. My tears are unrelenting. I try to keep myself together just for the sake of my children. Amelia is beside me waving her flag, and Elijah is sitting on my hip.

There are so many of them. They begin to march in and the gymnasium explodes. Every flag flies high and every heart is exposed.

They continue to march, to parade into the gym. Their presence is magnificent. They are a glorious sight to behold. They are proud, tired, worn, tan, strong, weak, scared, and ecstatic.

They stand at attention, and I can't help but wonder how many of them are absent. How many are left behind. How many came home too soon. I am humbled by their silence, by their camaraderie, by their stature, and by their determination to finish what they started. I have no idea what the guest speaker is saying. No idea what is happening around me. I can only stare at the uniform and marvel at the beauty of what they all stand for.

I find David's tan face in the crowd, and I am overcome. He is beautiful and proud, defiant, yet humble. He ignores his orders to stand at attention and stare ahead. He is staring right at me, realizing he is home.

"Is Daddy there?" Amelia asks. I bend to her level and point to David. She waves her flag at him. "Hi, Daddy!" she screams. "Why are all daddies here?" she asks.

I will never be able to capture what is happening, what I'm feeling or he's feeling or what we are all a part of here, today. I can only stare and finally release and cry.

"You are dismissed," rings over the crowd and women and men scramble for each other. David runs toward us. Around me it's chaos, weeping, shouting, laughter. It is a menagerie of emotion. Men hold their unseen newborn babies. Women reintroduce themselves to their children. Kids ride high on strong shoulders. Long, passionate kisses and hugs surround me. I can only imagine they are longer and stronger than ever before.

As David makes his way through the crowd of individual reunions, his eyes are focused and stern. He sees nothing but us now. He pulls us close to him and holds us with his strong arms. "There is something I want to give each of you," he says.

He pulls away from us and begins to unfasten the pocket on his sleeve. I have come to expect gifts from him when he has been away. I smile and try to guess what he could have for us. "These are very special to me, and I want you to know how much I care about each gift."

I see the edging of lace and delicate yellow fabric, and my heart surges against my chest. He pulls the handkerchief from his pocket, folds it gently, and pushes it back into my hands. "I got it dirty," he says apologetically. "I carried it with me every day. It doesn't smell like you anymore." I put it to my nose and inhale everything about him. I smell dirt, sweat, gasoline, and the faint aroma of smoke. "I suppose it smells like me now. Sorry."

"It smells wonderful," I say. I pull him to me and press myself deep into his chest. I need to convince myself he is really here.

"And now, you two," he says as he takes Elijah from my hip. He pulls out of his pocket two tiny socks covered in dirt and sand. "I took Elijah's socks with me. They reminded me of his little feet." He hands the socks to Elijah and laughs as Elijah uses his chubby fingers to pull the socks apart.

"Me, Daddy," Amelia says. He bends down to meet her eager arms. "I have something very special for you." He reaches into his pocket one last time and pulls out the used Band-Aids Amelia sent to him. "My boo stickers!" she screams.

"Daddy didn't have to use them for any boo-boos," he says.

The three of them revel in each other's company, and I thank God that my family is whole again. "Let's go home, babe," David says to me.

"Wanna take Daddy home, Amelia?" Her tiny hands leave the security of my legs. She reaches for him. He pulls her into his strong arms, puts his desert hat on her head, wraps his arm around me, and attempts to walk away from Iraq.

The Invitation

Driving David home, I notice that other wives have painted their trucks with festive colors. They have sidewalk chalk crying out "I love you" leading into their houses; windows are festooned with red, white, and blue; and ribbons and balloons are everywhere. A woman down the street even bought her husband a new truck.

I didn't think of these things. Our truck doesn't have wonderful words of love on it; no "welcome home" or "we missed you." I wonder if I'm deficient. I bought groceries. I got things I knew he would like. Planned meals I know he has waited for. I didn't decorate, paint, or chalk anything, and the surprise that I have planned for him seems to pale in comparison. Still, it will have to do.

I get Elijah down for his nap and nervously arrange the tea set, putting out the feathers, the stuffed animals, the makeup, and the jewelry. I tiptoe into the living room to find David and Amelia snuggling on the couch. "I have a surprise for you two," I tell them and motion them my way. They follow me down the hall into her room.

"Daddy! It's a tea party!" Amelia squeals when she sees her room. She runs to her tea set, but David's heaving catches me off guard. I look into his eyes to see utter pain. He grabs me in a bear hug and cries into my shoulder. I have no idea if what I have done is good or bad. Have I reminded him of everything he has missed? Have I touched a nerve with him about how he feels about being a father?

He holds me for a long time. He cries with heaving sobs. He pulls away from me, wipes the tears, and walks into her room to have a party. I stay in the hall, peeping in, listening. I want to make sure he is okay. I need to make sure I haven't created an avenue for his destruction.

She wears the cowboy hat. He's in a lacy blue hat. She has pink feathers. He has blue feathers. They share tea and plastic fruit with a gorilla and a teddy bear. She is thrilled to be using a real tea set. He is thrilled for her.

Tears of joy and relief ease down my cheeks. Neither she nor David seems to notice that I'm watching, taking pictures, and videotaping. They only have eyes for each other, and right now, I only have eyes for them.

"Would you like more tea, Ms. Amelia?" he says.

"Yes," she says, holding out her cup. They giggle and laugh. I turn off the cameras and turn to leave. "Daddy? Daddy, you home?"

I leave him to his answer. It is a private conversation.

I step into the shower full of contentment. It is the first wave of peacefulness that I have felt in a long time. She will heal now that her questions about her father are answered. Finally there will be an end to her pain. I feel like I have helped her regain her footing. But I am still unsure of his reaction and of his tears.

I stay in the shower for a long time. I want to wash away the anger, tiredness, and resentment.

When I step out of the shower, they're still playing, still wearing makeup, still sporting hats and necklaces. Again my presence doesn't register, and I am thankful to have a few moments alone.

Elijah wakes, and the spell is broken. David tenderly puts Amelia's toys away. He tries to find where things go. He looks to me for help. He is not used to her having "big girl" things. He is not used to having a big girl.

She walks out of the room full of joy. I catch her and pull her down to the ground again. Only long enough for a hug. Then I set her free to float through the house as she wishes.

I look to him for an answer. "Are you okay?" I ask timidly.

"Yeah," he says. "I have always dreamed of having tea parties with my little girl." He fights new tears. "That was the best present you could have given me."

Assessing the Damage

As I lie with him on the couch, breathing in softly and slowly, it all begins to hit me just how much we have been through. We have crossed oceans, weathered months of separation, worked through deaths, births, holidays, pain, and suffering. David was attacked several times, and Amelia, Elijah, and I had to decide that every day was worth going through, worth pushing through, just to get one day closer to seeing him.

I watch him breathe, listen to his heart beating, and see the smile of contentment on his face. He has just put his babies down for a nap, and I am beside him tracing the edges of his curling mouth and watching his chest rise and fall. This is what he has waited for, what he has hungered for. He is able to touch his children again and to hold me in his arms.

But I am in turmoil. I cannot help but relive painful moments of what must have been a dream. It still seems to be my reality. I cannot seem to let go of the certainty that he will be leaving us again soon. Too soon. The deployments seem never-ending.

My mind flashes back to the pain. It has become so ordinary for us that it feels comfortable to stay in it. I feel the familiar pangs of weariness and resentment. I see David's eyes burning into me from the computer screen. I see him leaving us at the airport. I see the loneliness, the endless nights, and the inability to ever just relax and breathe. I see Amelia writhing in misery, her body flailing, crying, and collapsing from the agony of missing him.

I allow myself to fully see her now. For what she was feeling then. It is haunting to me. It is what keeps me from living in this moment with him. It is what keeps me from concentrating on his breathing and on his heart beating.

I am suffocating with some kind of overwhelming fear or turmoil that I just can't quite place. Not yet. It is pain that I know is there, but I am not quite sure where to file it. I close my eyes and try to listen.

Instead, I see and hear her banging her head on the floor. I hear her begging me to produce her daddy. I hear her screams. Over and over again. I feel every ounce of her pain weighing on me like bricks. It is devastating.

And I can't let go and concentrate on healing because it's the way I felt, and the way I continue to feel. I want to bang my head against the floor—both because I don't want him to leave again and because I can't stop thinking about him leaving again, and enjoy the fact that he is home with us today.

I lie next to him. He is home. He is breathing. His heart is beating. And I am tortured. I can't sleep. I can only see all that has happened playing in slow motion. I can see it for what it is, for what I could not before, for what I would not before.

The pain of Amelia's tears, the turmoil in David's eyes, the absence of Elijah's father, the emptiness in my heart, and the lifelessness of this house. I can feel it all, and I am not sure if my shoulders are broad enough. I am not sure if I can take any more than I have allowed. My body is weary and broken.

My heart won't stop pounding and my body can't just lie next to him and dream of where we are going and what will be for us tomorrow, waking next to him and seeing him play with his children. I try to focus on seeing his radiant and bursting smile. I try.

I cannot escape this torture, this fear, this ache, or this suffocating realness. I can only see her behind my eyes. I can only focus on her in pain and see her writhing in agony.

The torment doesn't end at the welcome-home ceremony. It doesn't end when he takes off his boots. It doesn't end with the joy in his face. It doesn't end with the happiness in Amelia and Elijah's faces. I am beginning to wonder if it ever ends.

Flickering Fuses

David says being angry and feeling out of control make him comfortable. It is almost like home for him. At least, what he called home for nearly a year.

He is tense, twisted, agitated, and easily frustrated. He has chest pains and his stomach is always in knots. He wakes at night, screaming. His dreams are full of blood, bombs, black smoke, charred remains, and terror. He drives slowly because he is constantly looking for bombs on the side of the road. He swerves violently when he sees garbage bags next to houses. They are full of imaginary explosives.

He avoids crowds. They make him uneasy. He hates loud noises. They make him fall to the ground and search for cover. He is quiet and angry. He doesn't smile, and he doesn't laugh. He can't smell Elijah and Amelia anymore. He could when he first came home. But the newness wore off, and now the smells of his past are emerging again. Now he can't smell anything pure or delicate. He can only smell the stench of burnt flesh. He can't see the blue in Elijah's eyes.

He can't see the playfulness of Amelia's. He can only see the open, scared, and lifeless eyes of the decapitated in Iraq.

He doesn't show his emotions around Amelia and Elijah. They are the only things that don't make him angry. But they do frustrate him. They hurt his ears with their screams. They pull on his nerves with their whining and constant chattering. They overwhelm him with the inability to be independent.

Dirty diapers repulse him. He is angered by their untidy eating habits. He cannot stand to feed Elijah or to watch his growing, messy hands learn to reward his mouth with pieces of bananas and pears. He is impatient with Amelia's desire to "do it myself." He is slow to warm and is frigid at times. And that frustrates him even more.

I want to help him. I would love to know how to help him. But I feel dead inside. I am unable to cry and I don't know how to sympathize. We are a lifeless pair. I look at him with longing. I want to hold him and comfort him and try desperately to do it. He can tell I am faking concern and compassion. And I hate myself for that.

I need help. Someone is going to have to dig deep inside me to find some glimmer of my emotion and to find what I really think and feel about this whole situation. I have been a stone for so long I can actually feel those edges inside me. That stone has become a comfortable abscess in my gut. It is friendly, comforting, and steadfast. It is dependable and unwavering.

I depend on my steadiness and frigidness because I can't depend on him. He becomes emotional over small things, angry over large things, frustrated over trivial things. I feel nothing.

I would love to say that it is only fear that I cannot touch or unhappiness that I can't feel. But I feel nothing. I am not happy, sad, or angry.

I want to sympathize, to understand and to give. I want to give more than I have. I would love to cry with him and to be angry with him. I have nothing. No shoulder for him. I am failing him, and I am disgusted with myself.

Bottled

I am no longer married to the happy-go-lucky man I once knew. I want to yell at him, to scream and beg him to be himself again. Can I somehow force him to be happy? I want him to laugh at my jokes and smile at me. I'd like to take on his pain, to handle it for him. It's not possible. I don't yell at him. I can't.

The rational side of me pushes me for patience. After all, I can't even remember what it is like to be myself. But, somehow I expect him to return to what he was before. I want him to be that man who camps on the side of a mountain. The one who has an infectious smile and laughs uncontrollably at nonsensical jokes. I want him to be the man who could relate to every child and could find the silver lining in every cloud. I want him to be who he can never be again. I want to be who I can never be again.

I just miss him. I miss him so much, and he is here sitting next to me holding my hand. He is functioning, but he is static. I need to beg him, to plead with him to snap out of it. But I don't yell, beg, or plead, because it won't help. At some point I will have to reacquaint myself with the man that I love. I need to court him again, to date him again and learn what makes him laugh, what makes him smile, and what makes him happy.

I am scared that they are things that will not make me laugh. What if they don't make me smile, or don't make me happy? What if we never return to each other? I am worried about us. And I want to tell him. But I don't tell him. Because I can't. There are no words. No way to voice my fears.

I try to leave it all alone. To keep telling myself that there is no need to rush him. Even though I know he could leave again. This love is stronger than us and we are meant to be. With that knowledge in the back of my mind, urging me forward, I set out to meet him, to greet him, and to accept him. I want to get to know him all over again.

It does cross my mind to leave him, to run away from such an emotional existence. I discard the fleeting idea immediately because I know it wouldn't be him I was leaving; it would be something much bigger, something that can't really be left behind: fear. Every now and then I want to flee from something so heavy and full of pain. But I chose this family. And I continue to choose this family. There will never again be a time when I leave him because this is hard. There will never be a time that I make him feel that pain on top of everything else he's been through.

So, I choose to stay. Because I can.

Licking My Wounds

This deployment is behind us and David has been home for some time now, but it doesn't feel over. I am stuck and stagnant. I want to move, to push forward. I want anything to change. Nothing does, and I can't understand why.

I still feel like I need to be harsh and I still feel the need to be protective of myself and not to let go of my feelings or my affection. I can hold the kids, love them, and kiss them. They have become my closest friends. But I can't kiss him, not without feeling like stone. Something is very wrong with me. I must be in shock. I am shocked. I am shocking.

This is supposed to be a time of release, a time to celebrate his return, to enjoy the feeling of family, but I feel short of breath. It is as if I have no breath. I am empty.

When he kisses me, I respond the way that I am supposed to: I kiss in return. "I love you." I say what I know to be true, but I can't feel what I know is there, what I know exists. I can't feel anything, and that panics me. My body knows it is over and registers that he is hugging me, but my mind can't let go. I can't let go of the tiredness. Or release the anger and the emptiness or the repetitive, robotic movements that got me through it all.

I want to be a loving person again, forgiving and open. My mind pushes me to find that once accepting, responsive and active listener. My heart yearns to be comforting and to be alive again. I want so much to return to the person that I was; the person that he loves. I want to be the person that I had learned to like, to accept, and to appreciate. This person is foreign to me. This person is cold in the mirror, lifeless and monotone.

My eyes are vacant and exhausted. They are bloodshot, lifeless. There are dark circles under my eyes, heavy bags, and new wrinkles. I look in the mirror, and I have no idea what I have become. I am now the stranger in our house.

At some point, I disconnected and just went through the motions. I sent letters, talked to him on the phone, typed on the computer, and sent packages. But when the reality of his deadly situation came home on a video, it caused me to detach. The thought of reconnecting is too much for me because I am terrified to really let him in. What if he goes to Iraq again?

I don't want to think about it anymore. And I don't want to continue to focus on what I missed, on what I feel like I deserve, or on what I feel like I am owed. It all feels too selfish. But I still feel cheated. Since David got home, I have been in the cloud of his depression. It is a cloud that I welcomed. It is one that I walked into myself and one that I would gladly stay in forever if it meant being with him. But at some point, it needs to be okay that I have needs, too. It needs to be known that I have a breaking point; I have been the rock for too long.

I feel guilty for leaving them for only minutes to do something for me. What if they need me? What if they cry? What if David needs me to help him? What if he needs to talk? I want to feel appreciated, to feel like my pain is allowed. To feel like anything I need to do to make myself feel more human, more cultured, or more aware of life will be welcomed.

It seems if I pretend I am okay, he believes it. I stay silent and steadfast while he continues to unwind and break free from his deployment. It is a game I have brought upon myself. I cannot expect him to see my broken pieces. His are shattered. I cannot expect him to put me back together. I cannot expect him to see my tired eyes when his are lifeless and blind to all that surrounds him.

I hate to think that I will not get over this deployment, and I hate myself for needing something. Especially when he needs something more. But I can't give it to him right now. I can't give it to anyone. I need something so deeply. I would beg for it, if I only knew what it was.

Bated Breath

Communicating with David suddenly becomes very easy for me. He doesn't want me to talk, he wants—he needs—me to listen. So I do. I listen. And I listen. I listen to story after story. I meet his eyes. I give him long, deep stares. He knows I am listening.

He talks about when his gunner was nearly killed by a sniper. I hear him describe the shattered glass and hear exactly how that bullet would have ripped through his friend's head and exploded his memories onto the concrete. He talks about blood, bombs, sand, mosques, and Iraqi society. His stories are violent, explosive, and shocking. He is overflowing with them.

I hear his torment, and when I push my needs and fears to the very back of my mind, we can actually talk about his pain, his fears. We are communicating very well about him.

We are worried for him, David and me, worried that he is going to have a breakdown at any moment. That he is going to lose his patience with the children. We are concerned that Elijah's cries are piercing to him. We are worried that Amelia's feistiness is too much.

I do all that I can to ease his transition. I feed, clothe, bathe, entertain, and discipline the children. I cook breakfast, lunch, and dinner. Clean the dishes and the house and give him every bit of space he needs to regain his footing. He isn't able to function in our society. Not yet. So I'm where I was six months ago, only now I have one more person to care for, and I need to care for him unconditionally. I know this.

I'm willing to do anything he needs. I console him and urge him to talk. I strain to listen and attempt to understand. And ignore the fact that my once steadfast husband is no longer available to me.

He has too much to release before he can become, once again, the husband and father we know him to be. Or take in my anger and worries. But all of it seems too overwhelming, or as though we are pushing something that may never be. He has time off from work, and I catch myself willing him to leave the house. I feel guilty for needing to return to what seems normal: life without him.

I try to reassure him that it doesn't matter, that he can do as he wishes. He can come into my life and share the running of it again. I am willing. I want him to feel strong and needed, wanted and necessary. But that doesn't mean it is easy to give up that control. And at some point, I will need to be heard and understood. I am not sure how long I can wait. Who deserves the sacrifice that he is making? Who is thanking him for it? Who is helping us get through this? We play house with each other, trying to coax an ounce of sanity back into our lives. We are on a waning timetable. We must find our way back to each other in a few short months because he will begin his training for his next deployment. We have to adjust, and readjust, and let go again.

I am angry about it. I don't want to be, but I am. This moment is supposed to wash over me like warm water, and I am frustrated that it isn't working out that way. I want to relish the warmth of his breath and the heat of his body. To wallow in the sound of his laughter. I want to bathe myself with the mere presence of his being.

But he will go again. I can't revel in his homecoming. It's temporary. I have to prepare myself for him to leave us again. With the war in Iraq raging on, the surge of troops increasing, and the deployments extending, there is little hope of keeping him here with us.

With Nothing Left to Give

With David home, I find one place to retreat: the shower. Each time I stand under the hot water, I hope it will make me feel alive again. One day I disappear under the faucet and turn the tap to hot. I want it scalding. I want to wash away everything that is polluting me. I turn the cold water off completely, and my skin begins to turn from white to pink and then to red.

I close my eyes and let my mind finally release and journey to the one place that it could not before. It is a place of white chairs and familiar people. I hear quiet music. It is a place of beautiful green grass and clear blue skies. It is a place of constant hugs and kisses. It is a place of crisp whiteness. It is a haven for open feelings and honest emotion. It is the burial plot of a soldier. David.

I look at the coffin. It is draped with a flag. It is the coffin I have feared, the coffin that has haunted me. Within it, my happiness and his wedding ring.

I sit there and try to breathe. I have no breath, no life. I can only moan. And cry. And wail.

I hear David running to the shower and feel him get in with me. His clothes are wet, and he is holding me. A muffled moan escapes that is both haunting and comforting. I feel shaking all around me, and his strong arms are under me. He struggles to keep me on my feet, and he begs me to tell him what is wrong.

"Melissa! Melissa! What is wrong? Are you hurt? Did you hurt yourself?" I can hear him screaming at me. He pushes me up. He is wet. The water bounces off his shoulders onto the wall. His eyes are full of concern. I can't breathe.

He lowers me to the floor of the tub. He sits behind me, holding me. Water covers us. I can only hear moaning. Only feel shaking. "Breathe. Breathe. Breathe." He whispers to me over and over again until I can finally respond.

I am breathing, shaking, moaning, crying, and feeling. Finally I am feeling. I am feeling more than I ever dreamed possible. I am feeling and crying and shaking and breathing. "Are you okay?" he asks.

I look up into his terrified eyes. "I'm fine," I whisper.

Amelia runs into the bathroom, and I immediately turn from her. I don't want her to see it. I don't want her to feel it. She has already felt too much.

"Mommy's fine, honey," he tells her. "Look at Daddy! He's all wet," he laughs. Laughter replaces her fear. He pulls me from the bathtub floor and steadies me. Steam fills the room. My skin burns from the torture of the water. I nod to him. He turns off the water and hands me a towel. David takes Amelia out of our bathroom, and I move slowly to the mirror. It is the same mirror that held a monster before. It is the one that introduced me to a stranger.

I move my eyes up my scalded body, up my pink neck, over my chin, across my lips, over my nose, and into my bloodshot eyes. I see redness, tears, and spidery scarlet veins. I see emotion, feelings, fear, love, concern, panic, adoration, and marriage.

"Thank you, God."

Great Awakening

After purging my pain in the shower, I can finally see what has come home to me. David is stronger, harder, softer, and familiar somehow. He is not as boisterous, but I feel more comfortable around him. I feel safer. He doesn't laugh like he used to, but he hugs stronger and longer.

He isn't the same man I knew, but I feel closer to him. Like I have known him for years or felt him since birth. There is something calm in him, something raging, and something quiet. I try not to analyze it. I just try to be with him. To walk with him, laugh with him, and see the children through his eyes.

He is focused, concentrated, and devoted to us. He is more devoted than I have ever seen a man. He refuses to leave us. Not even for a walk. Not for a drive. He will not leave the spot next to us. He turns down time with friends, and he stares deeply into my eyes when I talk. He asks me to stop doing laundry, stop reading, stop cooking, stop moving, and come outside to listen to the crickets with him. He sits next to me for hours. He is quiet, calm, and he never stops touching me. He is not the person I knew. He is not the fun-loving boy who left. Afghanistan changed him, but Iraq sculpted him.

He is manly and familiar. His eyes are calming, and his presence is reminiscent. It is almost like a memory of someone I once knew. I feel oddly quiet around him. I am eerily reflective and at peace.

As he moves through his day, sometimes he stops suddenly and just stares at me. There is something always on the tip of his tongue. But he doesn't say it. I'm not sure he knows what it is.

He avoids people if possible. But when my parents come to visit, David is elated to see them. He hugs them strongly, tightly, and closely. He has missed them and seeing them is making him feel more firmly rooted in his home. We play cards at night. We watch the kids. Amelia and Elijah are thrilled to have them. We are thrilled to have them. They are here to celebrate with us. This year is finally over.

Elijah's birthday is today. His party is outside, and I can't wait to give him the chocolate cake. He is oblivious to the people around him, and he is completely ecstatic about his presents.

David cooks, and I serve. I am mingling, talking, and visiting. David is not. He is not the social butterfly I once knew. He isn't dancing from person to person making sure that each is comfortable and well taken care of. He doesn't socialize or talk about sports.

He isn't laughing loud, boisterous laughs. But he is having fun, quietly. He stands protectively over Elijah's highchair. He isn't focused on anyone or anything but the smile exploding from Elijah's mouth. He laughs and smiles only for his son today.

Elijah smashes cake into his face, mouth, and nose. He is covered with delicious fudge. He pushes the cake around the tray, and icing drips from his nose and mouth. He looks from person to person and laughs his distinctive little giggle.

David stands alone, which is different, but it is somehow okay now. I watch him as he helps clean the mess. He and my father are talking, and I begin to piece together the puzzle that has confused me since David came home.

I can see it now between them. I see it through their knowing glances, unspoken words, and silent gestures.

It is camaraderie. When he looks at David, there is an understanding in my father's eyes that I have never been able to conjure. He looks at David with pride and respect. David returns the favor. When he talks to my father, there is peacefulness and calmness in David's eyes that I cannot create.

They sit at the table, talking, sharing stories, and understanding each other in a way that I never will. I cannot begin to understand or face what my father has seen or what he went through during the Vietnam War. I cannot fathom the horrific welcoming he received from America or the hate-filled words he heard.

I could not stomach hearing those things about David. I would not understand the person who said them. David and Dad talk, and as I watch them walk together, I finally begin to realize what it is about David that has become so comforting, so endearing, and so beautifully elusive.

It's sacrifice. It's knowing pain. It is the aura of someone who has changed forever. My father and now David have seen death. They have avoided it. They have fought for it. They have fought against it. They will never again know the innocence of their youth. They are comforted in each other's ability to understand.

Knowing how hard he fought to come home to us, I have no doubt David will make our lives together meaningful. It is for that reason I know my father is proud of him. And for that, I am immensely proud of my father. I only wish I could have seen it sooner.

I am lucky. I have had two heroes in my life.

Scar Tissue

Things are starting to feel normal. David is working again, and I am waiting for him to come home. I happily play with the kids and delight in cooking David's favorite foods. We know it is his hand on the turning doorknob at five o'clock. We are not holding our breath any longer. There is no invisible cloud around us.

But there is one lingering piece of the puzzle for David, a documentary about David and his fellow soldiers. Shyly David mentions it, wondering if I would be willing to watch with him. When I say I would be thrilled to see what he really did every day, he is excited to sit with me. He puts the documentary on, and we settle onto the couch to watch. We snuggle. It is a date. There are so many interviews. There are explanations of the missions and people talking about being proud to serve. They are proud to be in the Army. They are proud to do their part. David is proud, too. I can see it in his explanations of every second of the movie. "That is my truck. There! Can you see it moving through the street?" he asks. I look from truck to truck. They all look the same. "Oh, yeah. I see it," I say.

He stops the video to explain in more detail. He stops it to clarify. And he stops it when he is in the background, the foreground, or anywhere on the television. On the screen, he shoots his gun. I watch as he does his job and watch as he waits to do his job. With his gun in his hand, patrolling, he greets Iraqis on the street with a casual nod.

He is littered throughout the documentary, and I feel like he is almost a celebrity. I know this is a movie that may be seen only by those who were there, that no one will ever really see or notice that David is there or was there. Not unless he brings attention to the fact. I am sure I will be one of the only people ever to see it.

He doesn't tell me his interview is coming up. I only expect to see him working, or see him in the background. I can feel him get a little tense, a little excited. He fidgets next to me.

"Are you okay?"

His face is on the screen. Then it's over before I realize what happened. "Wait a minute! Rewind that," I say. He responds with laughter.

In his interview, he talks about how hard a deployment is and that his wife and his kids are what get him through. He describes us as his "heart, blood, and soul." I watch it again and again. He laughs while I make him rewind it, not to hear what he says, just to soak in the image of him there putting his heart on the line for all to see.

I should have assumed that would be his answer. I know we are his foundation. But hearing him say it makes me sit taller, prouder. And I am so proud to know him, to be his friend, to have married him, and to have had his children.

I am proud of our children, of Amelia's resilience and Elijah's ability to adapt. I am proud of myself, proud that I made it through, proud to have not accepted the invitation to move in with my parents.

I continue to rewind it over and over again. We both watch, our grins getting bigger and bigger. It finally feels over. We sit contentedly watching more of the movie.

Then David tenses, and begins to move away from me. "I can't watch this part," he informs me. But he does.

We watch as the soldiers one by one mourn their fallen "brothers" and friends. On screen, the men and women try to hold themselves together, try to be strong, and try not to let the grief and loss overtake them. Some of them can't. They cry and sob.

They salute empty boots and empty helmets. Dog tags dangle with no neck to give them life. Soldiers play taps on a bugle. They are stoic, quiet, reserved, and engulfed in their pain.

One man allows a single tear to escape. He does not wipe it away, but it's the only one to drop. Another man carefully hangs a framed photograph of a fallen soldier. He does so respectfully and lovingly. He makes sure she is secured to the memorial wall and holds her for a moment to steady her new place in his life.

It is amazing that these men and women make it through the day. It is astounding that they make it through the fear, through the sadness, and through the anger and frustration. They are each a marvel.

I look at David. He is quiet. I am not sure if I have ever witnessed such vivid emotion clouding a room. I have never been this close to it. I have never experienced something that completely humbled me. Not until this. My heart ached and nearly stopped when I tried to speak what could be our last goodbye, and I felt the thick emotion surrounding me at his welcoming ceremony, but those emotions were connected to me. They were what surrounded and humbled me at home. This emotion is raw, explosive, achingly expressed, and it is rarely witnessed by the people at home. This is their private moment as soldiers, captured for all to see. This is their moment of painful goodbyes.

Sitting next to me, David fights his desire to cry. His eyes well. I can't imagine what he has been through. Or what he will go through again. I cannot even pretend to know.

My end of this deployment has been full of challenges. But, I have not had to leave someone behind. I have not had to watch friends fall. Or question my integrity in this war. I have not had to wonder if my war is just or necessary or why my life is spared while another is taken. I have not had to worry for my safety or fight for my life. I have not had to wonder if what I am doing is right or wrong.

David is silent for a long time after the documentary is over. I have no idea what to say to him. So I say nothing. We sit on the couch until he is ready to move. And to his credit, he does move, and he continues to move. And to my amazement, he begins to smile again.

Taking Inventory

The tree outside my living room window bursts with fall. Yellow leaves dangle and drop from the limbs, and I watch from behind the glass as Amelia, Elijah, and David rake them into small piles.

Amelia struggles to rake as many leaves as her daddy. He gently covers her hands with his strong ones and shows her how to capture the leaves beneath her pink plastic rake. Elijah repeatedly bangs the ground with his blue rake, making me giggle. He pounds it, harder and harder each time. He smiles at his accomplishment, and David applauds his effort.

I walk through the maze of boxes in my house and examine everything just one last time. The movers will be here soon, and I want to make sure that they will know what goes with them and what stays with us. My eyes linger on my wedding dress, and I fight the urge to look through all of our photo albums. Amelia and Elijah have their favorite toys and puzzles prepared to leave, and their stuffed animals are poised and ready.

I chase both cats to put them in their travel cages and search the house for last-minute additions. I walk into Amelia's room to make sure her pink dolly has not been packed. She sits on Amelia's suitcase, and I notice that Amelia has pulled Little Daddy from the box of packed toys. He sits next to dolly, ready. He will ride with us, too. She hasn't asked about him for months. But he has been in the background, just in case.

We are leaving Fort Drum. We are moving to Tennessee, just outside Fort Campbell, Kentucky. David's next deployment date is already set. We will say goodbye again, wrap ourselves in pain and anger again, and we will struggle to rearrange our lives again when he comes home.

I try to push that familiar fear and worry from my mind, and I walk through my house and bid it farewell. I stop to stare at the floor where Amelia banged her head. I linger in front of the kitchen door where he told us goodbye for his first deployment. I touch the rolled rug where Elijah finally learned to crawl. I hover in the room that first smelled of babies. I stand in our bedroom and remember the first time we walked in there. I remember David's hands on the swell of my belly as we discussed where to put the bed and how to arrange the nursery. This was our first home as a family. It holds our laughter, joy, anger, goodbyes, reunions, and tears.

I hear a knock on the living room window, and I walk in to find their faces smashed against the glass. David motions for me to come outside. Beneath the tree is a pile of yellow leaves waiting to be demolished.

I walk outside to join my family. It is cold. My joints tighten and my cheeks tingle with the promise of a Fort Drum winter. "Mommy, look at our weaves!" She runs around and around the pile, too excited to contain herself. Elijah tries to mimic her, but his steps are still new and clumsy. He falls. And laughs. And falls again.

"They are dying to jump in these leaves!" David smiles and his cheeks are pink. "We have been waiting for you to watch," he says. I inhale the smell of leaves and pine. I take off my jacket and pull my fleece over my head. I have on a tank top, and I immediately begin to shake from the cold.

"Are you crazy? What are you doing?" David is shocked. I welcome the chill bumps on my bare arms, feel the cool breeze blowing through my hair and over my back, and pull the smell of fall into the depths of my lungs. I want to feel it all. To feel everything that is real and now. I don't want to think ahead to the deployment that waits for me, and I don't want to look back to the pain of the one behind me. I want to hear my children laughing, and I want to see my husband smiling.

I close my eyes, catch my breath, and jump.

Epilogue

"Nor love thy Life, nor hate; but what thou livst

Live well, how long or short permit to Heav'n."

—**John Milton,** *Paradise Lost*

Filling Every Space

The trees in Tennessee are towering and welcoming. They blossom, sway in the wind, and offer their beautiful colors in ways that the trees at Fort Drum never could. They thrive in the warm sun and stretch to the sky with radiant branches in thick forests of plush green. They offer peace and comfort. They offer breathtaking scenery and a renewed sense of hope.

Our new house has no bare floors, and Elijah finally has a room to call his own. We reclaimed our bedroom, and our backyard is full of toys, a sandbox, and a play set. Birds chirp outside our window, and warm summer and light winter breezes remind me that life still moves and continues to circulate. Everything smells sweeter and fresh, here, away from the painful memories of Fort Drum. Even the low-flying Army helicopters training above our house can't make me return to the frigid memories of upstate New York.

It has been over a year since we left the desolate trees of Fort Drum. When the moving truck pulled away from our driveway, it took with it the pain, loneliness, and desperation that clutched and held me captive. I never looked back. Only forward to what a new home, a new base, and a new perspective could bring.

David left it behind, too. Once we moved, he no longer found the kids annoying or loud. He reveled in their laughter again, and he carried them on his shoulders while they giggled and squealed. They waited for him at the window when he was due home, and they ran to him and jumped into his open arms. He had become, once again, the daddy that Amelia mourned and begged for. And for Elijah, he became the light and joy in the room.

But there were still traces of the deployment buried within him. They will most likely be a part of him for the rest of his life. At times, he still awoke at night. Sometimes screaming. He still had chest pains, and he still searched for a way to push images of dead bodies and charred remains from his head. They haunted him. He went to counseling, but there was little that could be done. He was fine. As fine as someone could be coming home from war.

Amelia recovered as much as possible. It took her several months to fully believe that he was with us again. "Daddy, you going back to work?" she asked for months. With each "No" she heard, a piece of her pain lifted. Some of her anger lingered, but she still fell into his arms with little resentment. She asked about her old home and her old room, but the happy moments of tea parties and long story sessions in her new pink room with David began to ease those images from her mind.

Elijah only grew more attached to David. They spent hours playing with soccer balls and matchbox trucks. David took him for long walks around our neighborhood, and Elijah tried desperately to take large steps just like his daddy. He walked for hours with David until his little legs could handle no more. When David returned carrying Elijah on his shoulders, I always knew that they were well traveled.

I wish I could say David is with us now, enjoying the scenery and the infectious laughter of the kids. But he is gone. Again. Thankfully, he didn't leave for Afghanistan with his unit. Instead, he went to train to become an officer. For ten to twelve months.

So, we are alone again, and I find myself in familiar territory. Elijah, now two, stands at the window asking for him, just as

Amelia did a little over a year ago. I see her chubby hands in his as he spreads them on the window, and I hear her familiar cries of "Want Daddy!" coming from his tiny mouth. Once again, David visits our world on the web cam, and she twirls for him in front of the camera. Her legs are longer, thinner, and her words are sharp and witty. "See how I twirl very so beautifully?" she asks his face.

"You are a lovely dancer, Amelia," he replies.

She hugs the screen and kisses the monitor. He hears her affection, and he puts his lips to his web cam. "I really, really, love you, Daddy," she says.

Elijah vies for David's attention and he pushes Amelia out of the way. She lets him. "Look me, Daddy," Elijah says. He does no sort of twirling or dancing. He only demands to be seen by David.

"I see you, Bubby," David says. Elijah smiles and bounces up and down before he runs across the room, kicking, jumping, and flipping.

We function and continue as a family in the only way we know how. He calls when he can, and we don't stop living to wait for him. Amelia paints detailed pictures of stick figures, and she now signs her name at the bottom in distinct letters. Elijah sends David "e-mails" full of finger paint and stickers. We take bulky packages and chocolate-smeared letters to the post office.

And they delight in his letters to them. They sit excitedly on the couch as I read them details of Daddy's "camping trips" and fabricated stories about David's roommate. He sends handmade cards and folded paper airplanes. They hold them and play with them with pure joy and adoration. When the excitement of each new letter dwindles, Amelia takes it and places it in a special box hidden in her drawer. She thinks that I have no idea it exists.

"This is a special box just for you," David told her before he left. "You can put secret letters and stories in it. It is a special box just between you and me."

They watch their new "Daddy movie" throughout the week. The old one, worn and broken, didn't make it to Tennessee. They sit, side by side, on the floor and watch and laugh as David falls while playing a game of Twister. They follow along in their books while

David reads about ballerinas, dogs, and baseball. They listen as he plays with their puppets, toys, and stuffed animals.

Elijah is now the one holding and letting go of my hand at gymnastics as we move around the obstacle course. He flips, flails, and falls into a rolling ball of laughter. He does handstands and wraps his body around the uneven bars. He is independent and boisterous. He has no reservation about the balance beam. His tiny feet move across the beam with lightning precision. He stops at the end, looks back to me, and giggles as he jumps off the end and collapses in a ball on the cushioned mat below. He pops up, looking to me for praise, and I readily and happily provide it.

Amelia now moves and flips on her own. I watch her across the gym while Elijah tumbles and plays. She isn't timid anymore, and she has little friends who laugh, jump, and cheer with her. Her legs move swiftly and surely across the beam, and I can't help but remember her once tiny hand on mine as she timidly moved across the beam. Now her hands grip the narrow wood as she attempts a handstand without her coach. She looks to see if I am watching. She finds me in the moving crowd. "Mommy! Did you see?" she screams at me.

"Of course I did, baby," I respond. She waves to me and joins her friends in line. My heart swells with pride to see them both evolving, and I feel that familiar pang: I wish David could see this.

At night, I lie awake again, thinking of him. The bed feels enormous, and I think about sleeping on the couch. But I don't. His unread books sit on the nightstand, waiting to be read. His pillow guards his vacant side of the bed. His clothes, cologne, toothpaste, and shampoo keep idle in their spots. And I lie in our bed, waiting for him to come home.

When he does come home, we will pack and move again. And he will leave us again. There is a promise of a new base, and we will have to wrap our things again, pack our memories again, and prepare our children for a new house and another deployment. With his school and the next deployment combined, he could be gone for twenty-five months. If I linger on the thought, it suffocates me. I have only barely begun to realize the pain that my heart and mind endured while he was in Iraq. I don't know how any heart could take more deployments.

For now, I look to my children. They are functioning, happy in their present home, and learning to live with a father who adores them and is rarely home. Little Daddy still keeps watch over Amelia's room. He will always be there, should she need him. But she is learning to live without him. I am learning how to deal with it, too. This time, I don't keep the television on to fool myself into believing the buzzing sound is really David in another room. I don't dread the silence. And I don't wish away the moments that we are without him. It is what it is.

We sit at the table eating dinner, the three of us, and I listen as the kids chat and giggle with each other. Amelia pretends to feed her stuffed animal her cold broccoli. Elijah laughs uncontrollably as Amelia scolds her pink dog for not eating what she has cooked. I laugh to myself as I hear my words leaving her mouth. Elijah pretends to feed his penguin as well. He follows her lead.

We talk about gymnastics, trips to the library, and constant conversations about David. What his latest letter said. The vacation we will all take when he comes home. The funny stories he told on the phone. We talk, and talk, and talk about him. It is the one lesson I have painfully learned. Talking about him and thinking of him is the only way to keep him fluid and present in our lives. If I try to avoid his absence, it only causes more pain.

We continue to go on with our days, and with our lives, with the realization that we are still a family. We are just a family divided, and always waiting. Waiting to see his face on the computer, or for him to call, or to get his letters. Our days aren't flooded with tears or fear. There is no worry about when or if he will come home. There are no terror-filled days. Only the desire to move time until he comes home again. It is there, in the back of my mind. The realization that we will have to submerge ourselves in another deployment, another year of pain and suffering. But I dull it with laughter and fun-filled days.

Not that we don't have moments. I do still long for him and still touch the empty space on his pillow. Sometimes Amelia still cries out for him in her sleep. And, Elijah does stand at the window, every so often, looking for David's familiar walk and uniform coming up the driveway. But when he does, I have a sweet angel who remembers the pain of before. She remembers the waiting, the tears, and the head-banging. Somehow, she still remembers. And she goes to Elijah when he cries. She covers his little shoulders with her delicate arm. And she attempts to calm him with her sweet voice. "I miss Daddy, too, Eli. It is okay to be sad," she says as she hugs him. "I will help you."

She takes my breath. I am amazed by her courage and strength. I try to stay back, to stay out of their conversation about their daddy. "I am here. I will play with you and make you laugh," she tells him. And she does. She runs around and bounces up and down until his tears leave his face. "Gank you, Mia," he tells her. "Sure," she says casually.

I thought I would be angry again. Or depressed. But I feel none of that. I am thankful he isn't in Baghdad, patrolling the streets and writing of his attacks. I am content in my quiet nights and child-filled days. I am peaceful in our separation and our life. I have to be. I can't think of what is ahead, or of the pain behind. I choose, instead, only to concentrate on the husband who hates to leave my side and who loves me "more every day," and the children who need me to be happy, content, and strong. His laughter echoing through the house from the computer speakers and their infectious smiles are all I need. They are, when it is all said and done, all that matters.

Acknowledgments

Thank you Chris, Beverly, Angela, Wyona, Jodi, April, Aunt Mary Ann, and every other military spouse that has ever stayed behind, waiting. Your strength is grounding, and your will, ironclad. You are the guts and foundation of the military, and for that, I am deeply proud to know and stand beside you.

This book would not exist without the dedication, and willingness to take a second look, of my agent, Kate Epstein. Thank you, Kate, for believing in me and in the story behind the words. A special thank you to my editor, Ann Treistman for seeing where the book could go and for actually taking it there. Thank you, Rose Carrano for your dedication and willingness to always be available to me. Thank you, LeAnna Weller Smith for creating such a personal and wonderful cover.

Thank you to all my friends who are always willing to support me, no matter what. I love you. Without my family, this book would have never been possible. Thank you, every single one of you. Your love and support never cease to amaze me. Thank you, my sweet,

sweet parents, for always being there for me. Even when I didn't deserve it. Thank you, Keri, for the endless nights that turned into early mornings of listening, and for taking everything I threw at you. I owe you one, still. Thank you, Dr. Steven Carter for your guidance and willingness to help me get started. Thank you, Dr. Barbara Burch for taking such an early look and for always supporting me. Thank you, Dr. Rosemary Allen for making me believe, ten years ago, that a book was within me.

Thank you, Amelia and Elijah for blessing me in every possible way. Thank you for choosing me, and thank you for your endless love and infectious laughter. Without you, I cease to be.

And, David, there are no words that could ever express my gratitude to you. Thank you will have to suffice. So, thank you for my life. My greatest accomplishment will always be finding you. On that hot, summer night, my life began. Always, and in all ways, thank you.